T0154120

Praise for
Men Pray:
Voices of Strength, Faith, Healing, Hope and Courage

"A much-needed interfaith anthology.... A splendid resource for any man seeking insight and encouragement on the adventure of drawing closer to God."
—**Carl McColman**, author, *The Big Book of Christian Mysticism*
and *Answering the Contemplative Call*

"Many of these men's prayers took my breath away, too many to fully list. A wonderful and very masculine (and very personal) collection of the ways men approach God."
—**John Lionberger**, author, *Renewal in the Wilderness:*
A Spiritual Guide to Connecting with God in the Natural World

"Invites the reader to pray with men ancient and con-temporary, poetic and straight-forward, from differing faith traditions. This gathering of prayers represents a wide range of devotional practice and language; a fine resource for the life in the Spirit."
—**Mary C. Earle**, Episcopal priest and spiritual director;
author, *Celtic Christian Spirituality: Essential Texts Annotated and*
Explained and *Marvelously Made: Gratefulness and the Body*

"At my first reading of *Men Pray* I felt delight, at my second read the boundaries of my faith expanded, and then at my third reading I prayed those prayers. You might also."
—**Reb Zalman Schachter-Shalomi**, author,
Davening: A Guide to Meaningful Jewish Prayer and
Jewish with Feeling: A Guide to Meaningful Jewish Practice

Men
Pray

Men
Pray

Men Pray

Voices of Strength, Faith, Healing, Hope and Courage

Created by the
Editors at SkyLight Paths

With Introductions by
Brian D. McLaren

Walking Together, Finding the Way®

SKYLIGHT PATHS®
PUBLISHING
Woodstock, Vermont

Men Pray:
Voices of Strength, Faith, Healing, Hope and Courage

2013 Hardcover Edition, First Printing
© 2013 SkyLight Paths Publishing
Introductions © 2013 by Brian D. McLaren

For information regarding permission to reprint material from this book, please write or fax your request to SkyLight Paths Publishing, Permissions Department, at the address/fax number listed below, or e-mail your request to permissions@skylightpaths.com.

Library of Congress Cataloging-in-Publication Data

Men pray : voices of strength, faith, healing, hope, and courage / created by the editors at SkyLight Paths ; with introductions by Brian D. McLaren.
    p. cm. -- (Walking together, finding the way)
 Includes bibliographical references and index.
 ISBN 978-1-59473-395-6
1. Men--Religious life. 2. Men--Prayers and devotions. 3. Prayer. 4. Worship.
I. SkyLight Paths Publishing.
 BL625.65.M46 2013
 204'.330811--dc23

                        2012041835

10 9 8 7 6 5 4 3 2 I

SkyLight Paths Publishing is creating a place where people of different spiritual traditions come together for challenge and inspiration, a place where we can help each other understand the mystery that lies at the heart of our existence.

SkyLight Paths sees both believers and seekers as a community that increasingly transcends traditional boundaries of religion and denomination—people wanting to learn from each other, *walking together, finding the way.*

Manufactured in the United States of America
Cover and Interior Design: Tim Holtz
Cover Photos © Kellie Folkerts/Fotolia.com and © Galyna Andrushko/Fotolia.com

SkyLight Paths, "Walking Together, Finding the Way," and colophon are trademarks of LongHill Partners, Inc., registered in the U.S. Patent and Trademark Office.

Walking Together, Finding the Way®
Published by SkyLight Paths Publishing
A Division of LongHill Partners, Inc.
Sunset Farm Offices, Route 4, P.O. Box 237
Woodstock, VT 05091
Tel: (802) 457-4000   Fax: (802) 457-4004
www.skylightpaths.com

"Sorrowful" Tuesdays need not be without hope. Jesus knew what awaited Him and He knew He needed His Father. And so He prayed. Whether in our favorite prayer garden, our backyard, in our car, or in front of the Blessed Sacrament, we are called to pray—to raise our hearts and minds to God. Jesus showed us: Real Men Pray.

DAVID N. CALVILLO,
REAL MEN PRAY THE ROSARY, INC.

Contents

Introduction   xi

Faith   1

Courage   35

Healing   59

Strength   89

Hope   115

Acknowledgments   152

About the Contributors   153

Credits   159

Index of First Lines   164

Introduction

When I was a boy, I had a special love for my Grandpa Smith. He was funny. He did tricks. He sometimes took his false teeth out, which truly amazed my cousins and me. He had lots of tools and could fix anything. He could play ragtime songs on the piano. He told amazing stories. He radiated goodwill and the simplest, purest love.

And my Grandpa Smith loved to pray.

When he prayed, it felt like the world slowed down. His prayers filled a room with things that to me, a small boy, were magical and rare: humility, reverence, sincerity, honor, dignity, love. In my grandfather's presence, I knew there was a place for these things in the world. I knew, through him, they were real.

When my grandmother was dying through a slow, debilitating illness, I remember my grandfather crying when he prayed for her. I hadn't seen many men cry.

After her death, I remember visiting him once and staying at his home—just me and Grandpa. I think I was twelve or thirteen. I can't remember why this happened—my parents and brother may have stayed with an aunt in the area so he didn't have the burden of cooking and cleaning. Maybe everyone thought it would be nice for me to keep Grandpa company.

Everything is murky in my memory until this: I awoke to the smell of coffee. I followed the aroma into the kitchen where Grandpa's old-fashioned percolator was on the stove, brown brew splashing up into a glass bubbler. I don't think I had ever had more than a sip of the bitter liquid before, but it seemed right to accept when Grandpa offered me a cup.

I think he made toast—white toast with melted butter. I think he made poached eggs. I remember it being a little awkward—we had never eaten a meal together before, just the two of us; he had probably not often cooked for anyone but himself since Grandma's death. She was always the cook.

I remember us chatting about his garden. Then I remember him saying, "After breakfast, I always pray. Would you mind if I pray?"

"Of course not, Grandpa."

He went over to a counter and reached for something hidden behind the toaster. He came back with a little spiral notebook, as I recall, and out of its edges lots of other scraps of paper were hanging out—an envelope with a name in his scrawl, a napkin, a typed letter from someone, a torn sheet of typewriter paper. He also had a little book of missionaries, organized under countries, with their pictures and some information about them.

He began with thanksgiving ... a simple expression of gratitude for life and breath, for health and strength, for this new day, for the joy of having his grandson with him. He thanked God for the many years of happiness he shared with Grandma, and for his daughters and sons-in-law and grandchildren.

Then he opened his notebook and I saw all the names of my cousins. He prayed for us all, name by name. He flipped a page—prayer requests for his church, for the needy and infirm. He flipped through some more pages and prayed for the president and "all those in authority," for farmers and their need for rain, for orphans and widows, for Christians suffering persecution in communist countries. Then he went through the scraps of paper—almost like a bookkeeper counting receipts. Each scrap stirred a memory of someone who asked him to pray for them and whom he promised he would. He kept his promise. Finally he came to the missionary book and I remember thinking how impressive it was that this man who had only an eighth-grade education had interests in Bhutan, Bolivia, Burma, and Burundi. "Bless these missionaries. Protect their children. Provide for their financial needs. Give them good success in their hospitals and schools and churches."

I think the ritual lasted five minutes. It ended something like this: "And dear Heavenly Father, I thank you again that I could share these moments in your dear presence with my grandson, Brian. It's not easy being alone, and I know you sent him here to bless me with his good company this day. Amen."

I'm not sure why this memory brings tears to my eyes all these years later. Of course, I miss that wonderful man who filled a special place in my young life—a place that I now hope I can fill for my grandchildren.

I'm also touched because I feel somehow—intuitively, in my gut—that the man I am today was somehow shaped and is still in some way upheld by my name passing over Grandpa's lips at his kitchen table, morning after morning, though after all these years I can't claim to understand exactly how prayer "works."

My grandfather didn't seem to be bothered by all those theological questions of how prayer functions, of what prayer accomplishes, of how the prayers of one person interact with the free will of another or with "the sovereign will of God" or "the laws of nature." He didn't seem the type to question why prayer should be necessary, why an all-knowing God should need to be informed or why an all-benevolent God would need to be invited or coaxed into doing the right thing. Somehow, he flew above or below the altitude at which those questions buzz and bother.

Maybe that is part of what touched me so much that morning too.

Whatever else was going on as he bowed his head at that kitchen table, I think my Grandpa Smith was showing me something about what a good man, a true man, a real man, is.

A true man, he showed me, feels a share of responsibility for the world. He sees and hears and feels the needs of others and remembers them. He takes them to heart, and carries them—aided, if need be, by an overflowing spiral notebook and an old yellow pencil. A good man, he made clear, is a compassionate man, a tender man, a generous man.

But a good man also knows the needs that surround him are too great for him to carry alone, so he shares them with God, whose heart is ever bigger, whose capacities to help are ever greater than his own.

In some way, he showed me, a good man carries the needs and wounds and burdens of the world in his own heart and also shares them with another heart, that infinite well of compassion and power whose height and width and length and depth cannot be fathomed.

Now I know a Buddhist wouldn't say it exactly that way. Nor would a Hindu. Nor would an atheist. But I also suspect that if they had a Grandpa like mine, they'd know that however it is articulated, there is something real and profound to what I'm saying; something holy and wise beyond all articulations.

Why Do Men Need to Pray?

For our own well-being and survival, to be sure. There are times known to all of us when what life demands of us—patience, courage, wisdom, forgiveness, backbone—goes beyond the resources we can muster. We will either collapse or snap under the gravity of those demands, or we will open ourselves to a source of strength beyond our own to bear up under them.

We men also know there are times we have failed—miserably failed "in thought, word, or deed, by what we have done and by what we have left undone," as the old confession puts it (Book of Common Prayer, "Confession of Sin"). We know that if we are not to be sucked down into a vortex of guilt and regret, or if we are not going to slide into an addictive pattern of repeat performances, we need a kind of prayer where we can inventory our wrongs, process our remorse, and break up with the "me" we have been in the past so as to become someone better in the future.

But beyond our own well-being and survival, I think men need to pray so that our children and grandchildren and their peers will see what I saw in my Grandpa Smith's kitchen that day, and what I saw at all those Thanksgiving dinners and other occasions when we turned to him to "say the grace" or "offer a prayer."

If men like us don't pray, where will emerging generations get a window into the soul of a good man, an image of the kind of man they can aspire to be—or be with—when they grow up? If men don't pray, who will model for them the practices of soul care—of gratitude, confession, compassion, humility, petition, repentance, grief, faith, hope, and love? If men don't pray, what will men become, and what will become of our world and our future?

So I hope you will appreciate this book as I do: a needed resource that can help men pray.

What You Will Find within These Pages

My grandfather was a Christian, as am I, but the prayers in this volume, though all by men, span a wide range of religious traditions and historical settings. That variety provides many benefits—among them, a window into the soul of praying men you might not normally know. The prayers come in a variety of forms: poetry, prose, reflections, meditations, rituals.

They're loosely organized around needs we men face—courage, faith, healing, hope, strength. Together, they give us a window into the soul of praying men, and through that window they provide many glimpses into the sacred and divine mystery that no man can claim to fully grasp, control, or know ... but that any man can humbly approach as my grandfather did each morning at his kitchen table.

Who Should Read This Book?

You may be a man who has never prayed. In these pages you'll find the prayers of others upon which you can model your own. They can be like training wheels to help you learn to become a praying man yourself.

You may be a man who has prayed in the past but has lost the knack. Here you will find prayers that have the capacity to jumpstart your praying heart.

You may be a man who has only prayed within one tradition, and you want your prayer life to be enriched by sincere prayers from other traditions.

You may be a man who is sometimes asked to pray in public, and you wouldn't mind having some fresh material at hand for the next time that happens.

You may even want to keep this book by your toaster and let it be a companion to your morning coffee.

BRIAN D. MCLAREN

FAITH

A great British "metaphysical poet," a great Hindu mystic from India, two brilliant Christian apologists—one Protestant and one Catholic—a teenage Jewish boy with Asperger's syndrome, a Sufi genius, a Native American honoring the Great Spirit ... what do they all hold in common?

They all share the experience of faith. Even though the content of their faith may differ, and even though they would describe the object of their faith in different ways, they all participate in the experience of faith. And what a varied and complex experience that is ... spanning the pang of doubt, the rise of devotion, the elevation of reverence, the sense of humility in the presence of ungraspable grandeur, the thrill of "something more" that comes to us as an unexpected gift, the humbling awareness of need, the energizing feeling of unexplainable confidence.

Jesus famously said that it doesn't take a lot of faith to get started on the path of prayer. It only takes faith the size of a tiny mustard seed (Luke 17:6). "You don't need a whole lot," we used to sing in an old spiritual. "Just use what you've got." These prayers can help you do just that.

Prayer

Prayer changes at every moment in proportion to the degree of purity in the soul and in accordance with the extent to which the soul is moved either by outside influence or of itself. Certainly the same kind of prayers cannot be uttered continuously by any one person. A lively person prays one way. A person brought down by the weight of gloom or despair prays another. One prays another way when the life of the spirit is flourishing, and another way when pushed down by the mass of temptation. One prays differently, depending on whether one is seeking the gift of some grace or virtue or the removal of some sinful vice. The prayer is different once again when one is sorrowing at the thought of hell and the fear of future judgement, or when one is fired by hope and longing for future blessedness, when one is in need or peril, in peace or tranquility, when one is flooded with the light of heavenly mysteries or when one is hemmed in by aridity in virtue and staleness in one's thinking.

ST. JOHN CASSIAN

Give me all of you!!! I don't want so much of your time, so much of your talents and money, and so much of your work. I want YOU!!! ALL OF YOU!! I have not come to torment or frustrate the natural man or woman, but to KILL IT! No half measures will do. I don't want to only prune a branch here and a branch there; rather I want the whole tree out! Hand it over to me, the whole outfit, all of your desires, all of your wants and wishes and dreams. Turn them ALL over to me, give yourself to me and I will make of you a new self—in my image. Give me yourself and in exchange I will give you Myself. My will, shall become your will. My heart, shall become your heart.

C. S. LEWIS

Bitter-Sweet

Ah, my dear angry Lord....
I shall bewail, approve,
I shall complain yet praise,
And all my sour-sweet days
I shall lament and love.

GEORGE HERBERT

The Day of Gifts

It's not true that Your saints have won everything:
  they left me with sins enough.
Someday I'll lie on my deathbed, Lord, ill-shaven
  and yellow as a lifelong drunk.
And I'll make a general examination of myself,
  looking back over all my days,
And I'll see that I'm rich after all, ripe and rich
  with evil in its unnumbered paths and ways.
I haven't lost one single chance, Lord, to make
  matter for You to pardon.
Now I hearten myself with vice, having long ago
  sloughed off virtue's burden.
Each day has its own kind of crime, plain to see,
  and I count them like some paranoid miser.

If what you need, Lord, are virgins, if what you
  need are brave men beneath your standard;
If there are people for whom to be Christian
  words alone would not suffice,
But who know rather that only in stirring
  themselves to chase after You is there any life,
Well then there's Dominic and Francis, Saint
  Lawrence and Saint Cecilia and plenty more!

But if by chance You should have need of a lazy
   and imbecilic bore,
If a prideful coward could prove useful to You,
   or perhaps a soiled ingrate,
Or the sort of man whose hard heart shows up in
   a hard face—
Well, anyway, You didn't come to save the just
   but that other type that abounds,
And if, miraculously, You run out of them
   elsewhere ... Lord, I'm still around.

And what kind of a man is so crude that he
   hasn't held a little something back from You,
Hasn't in his free time fashioned something
   special for You,
Hoping that one day the idea will come to You
   to ask it of him,
And maybe this little that he's made himself, kept
   back until then, though horrid and tortuous,
   will please Your whim.
It would be something that he'd put his whole
   heart into, something useless and malformed.
Just like that my little daughter once, on my
   birthday, teetered forward with encumbered arms
And offered me, her heart at once full of timidity
   and pride,

A magnificent little duck she had made with her
   own two hands, a pincushion, made of red
   wool and gold thread.

   PAUL CLAUDEL

A noble and God-like character is not a thing of favor or chance, but is the natural result of continued effort in right thinking, the effect of long-cherished association with God-like thoughts.

JAMES ALLEN

As Kingfishers Catch Fire

As kingfishers catch fire, dragonflies draw flame;
As tumbled over rim in roundy wells
Stones ring; like each tucked string tells, each
    hung bell's

Bow swung finds tongue to fling out broad its
    name;
Each mortal thing does one thing and the same:
Deals out that being indoors each one dwells;
Selves—goes itself; *myself* it speaks and spells,
Crying *What I do is me: for that I came.*

I say more: the just man justices;
Keeps gráce: thát keeps all his goings graces;
Acts in God's eye what in God's eye he is—
Chríst. For Christ plays in ten thousand places,
Lovely in limbs, and lovely in eyes not his
To the Father through the features of men's faces.

GERARD MANLEY HOPKINS

On Theodicy

You are One split into many.
I am one of those many
You are a side of me.
Am I a side of You?
I like to think so.

JACOB HAIGH, age 13

On Theodicy

We gladly confess: "The eyes of all look to you, and you give them food in due season. You open your hand, satisfying the desire of every living thing."

That we gladly and confidently confess—

And yet, we notice your creatures not well fed but mired in hunger, poverty, and despair.

And yet, we notice the power of evil that stalks the best of us: the power of cancer, the dread of war, sadness of death—"good death" or cruel death.

And so we pray confidently toward you, but with footnotes that qualify. We pray confidently, but we will not deny in your presence the negatives that make us wonder.

We pray amid our honest reservations, give us patience to wait, impatience to care, sadness held honestly, surrounded by joy over your coming kingdom—and peace while we wait—and peace at the last, that we may be peacemakers and so your children.

We pray in the name of your firstborn Son, our peacemaker.

WALTER BRUEGGEMANN

Who Is the You I Pray to?

Who is the *you* I pray to?
Is it some extraterrestrial being
I'm addressing when I say "Lord?"
Is it some mega-size he or she,
some humanized projection
of my personal wants, god in my image,
the future of my own illusion?
Is this *you* some amalgam of our national
fantasies to protect a lifestyle
impossible for the rest of the planet?
Whatever "it" is, this god has to die,
or has already died. For surely
the Genesis of true religion
says we're created in the image of God,
male and female, God created them.

What if the *you* I pray to
is my higher self—the Christ self,
the ideal human hope for a Love Supreme
that can only take shape in the web
of interconnectedness with all my relations,
my human siblings and the rocks and rivers
mountains and deserts, glaciers and oceans?

What if the *you* I pray to
is at the same time you and us and me and we,
the yearning to be free to love? What if such
a web is the all-surrounding string-theory
universe that stretches out and in
and through—within all things,
the primal Love Force in whom we live
and move and have our being?

KENT IRA GROFF

The Mission of My Life

God has created me to do Him some definite service. He has committed some work to me which He has not committed to another. I have my mission. I may never know it in this life, but I shall be told it in the next. I am a link in a chain, a bond of connection between persons. He has not created me for naught. I shall do good; I shall do His work. I shall be an angel of peace, a preacher of truth in my own place, while not intending it if I do but keep His commandments. Therefore, I will trust Him, whatever I am, I can never be thrown away. If I am in sickness, my sickness may serve Him, in perplexity, my perplexity may serve Him. If I am in sorrow, my sorrow may serve Him. He does nothing in vain. He knows what He is about. He may take away my friends. He may throw me among strangers. He may make me feel desolate, make my spirits sink, hide my future from me. Still, He knows what He is about.

JOHN HENRY NEWMAN

The Circle of Life

Oh Great Spirit
Of the Indian People
Hear my words
For they are words that come
From the heart, soul and mind.
Oh Great Spirit
Be my mind,
Be my eyes,
Be my ears,
Be my heart,
Be my soul,
So that I may walk
With dignity and pride.
Oh Great Spirit
Of the Indian People
Know of me.
For I am of your people.
I am Indian,
An Indian of the Circle of Life
A prisoner of War
In my own Land!
Oh Great Spirit,
Of the Indian people,
Hear my words

For they are for you.
They are of you.
You are my way of life
In the Circle of Life.

LARRY KIBBY

The St. Francis Prayer

Lord, make me an instrument of your peace.
Where there is hatred, let me sow love.
Where there is injury, pardon.
Where there is doubt, faith.
Where there is despair, hope.
Where there is darkness, light.
Where there is sadness, joy.
O Divine Master,
Grant that I may not so much seek to be
    consoled, as to console;
To be understood, as to understand;
To be loved, as to love.
For it is in giving that we receive.
It is in pardoning that we are pardoned,
And it is in dying that we are born to Eternal Life.

Amen.

All My Senses

In one salutation to thee, my God, let all my
senses spread out and touch this world at thy feet.

Like a raincloud of July hung low with its burden
of unshed showers let all my mind bend down at
thy door in one salutation to thee.

Let all my songs gather together their diverse
strains into a single current and flow to a sea of
silence in one salutation to thee.

Like a flock of homesick cranes flying night
and day back to their mountain nests let all my
life take its voyage to its eternal home in one
salutation to thee.

TAGORE

Say Yes Quickly

Forget your life. Say *God is Great.* Get up.
You think you know what time it is. It's time to pray.
You've carved so many little figurines, too many.
Don't knock on any random door like a beggar.
Reach your long hand out to another door, beyond where
you go on the street, the street
where everyone says, "How are you?"
and no one says *How aren't you?*

Tomorrow you'll see what you've broken and torn tonight,
thrashing in the dark. Inside you
there's an artist you don't know about.
He's not interested in how things look different in the
    moonlight.

If you are here unfaithfully with us,
you're causing terrible damage.
If you've opened your loving to God's love,
you're helping people you don't know
and have never seen.

Is what I say true? Say *yes* quickly,
if you know, if you've known it
from before the beginning of the universe.

> RUMI

Frustration, Faith, and a Good Future

God, I'm frustrated.
Everything I touch turns into a muddle. I can't see if
this work is heading anywhere. I feel as if I'm turning
in circles. I'm tired and I'm tired of being tired.

So, here I am sitting with you for a moment, Creator
God. Once again, I recall your redeeming work in the
past—all those ancient stories—and I think of my
own life now. Is there still a purpose in my life, today?

I lift my eyes a bit higher. I look a bit farther. You
are the pioneer of our faith, already ahead of us.
Your good future is out there, both for me and for
this world you love.
God, I'll get up again.

I'll put my hand to the work that must be done.
Thank you for taking what I try to do and making it a
part of your good future, even if I can't see that today.

Time to get back at it!
And I know I'll meet you right back here, before
too long.

REV. DR. DANIEL BUTTRY

An Indian Prayer

My grandfather is the fire
My grandmother is the wind
The Earth is my mother
The Great Spirit is my father
The World stopped at my birth
and laid itself at my feet
And I shall swallow the Earth whole
when I die
and the Earth and I will be one
Hail The Great Spirit, my father
without him no one could exist
because there would be no will to live
Hail The Earth, my mother
without which no food could be grown
and so cause the will to live to starve
Hail the wind, my grandmother
for she brings loving, life-giving rain
nourishing us as she nourishes our crops
Hail the fire, my grandfather
for the light, the warmth, the comfort he brings
without which we be animals, not men
Hail my parent and grandparents
without which
not I

nor you
nor anyone else
could have existed
Life gives life
which gives unto itself
a promise of new life
Hail the Great Spirit, The Earth, the wind, the fire
praise my parents loudly
for they are your parents, too
Oh, Great Spirit, giver of my life
please accept this humble offering of prayer
this offering of praise
this honest reverence of my love for you.

H. KENT CRAIG

A Psalm

When psalms surprise me with their music
And antiphons turn to rum
The Spirit sings: the bottom drops out of my
    soul.

And from the center of my cellar, Love, louder
    than thunder
Opens a heaven of naked air.

New eyes awaken.
I send Love's name into the world with wings
And songs grow up around me like a jungle.
Choirs of all creatures sing the tunes
Your Spirit played in Eden.
Zebras and antelopes and birds of paradise
Shine on the face of the abyss
And I am drunk with the great wilderness
Of the sixth day in Genesis.

But sound is never half so fair
As when that music turns to air
And the universe dies of excellence.

Sun, moon and stars
Fall from their heavenly towers.
Joys walk no longer down the blue world's shore.

Though fires loiter, lights still fly on the air of
    the gulf,
All fear another wind, another thunder:
Then one more voice
Snuffs all their flares in one gust.

And I go forth with no more wine and no more
    stars
And no more buds and no more Eden
And no more animals and no more sea:

While God sings by himself in acres of night
And walls fall down, that guarded Paradise.

THOMAS MERTON

There were other joys to be found in their company, which still more powerfully captivated my mind—the charms of talking and laughing together and kindly giving way to each other's wishes, reading elegantly written books together, sharing jokes and delighting to honor one another, disagreeing occasionally but without rancor, as a person might disagree with himself, and lending piquancy by that rare disagreement to our much more frequent accord. We would teach and learn from each other, sadly missing all who were absent and blithely welcoming them when they returned. Such signs of friendship sprang from the hearts of friends who love and know their love returned, signs to be read in smiles, words, glances, and a thousand other gracious gestures. So were sparks kindled and our minds were fused inseparably, out of many becoming one.

SAINT AUGUSTINE OF HIPPO

Out of the silence at the beginning of time
you spoke the Word of life.
Out of the world's primeval darkness
you flooded the universe with light.
In the quiet of this place
in the dark of the night
I wait and watch.
In the stillness of my soul
and from its fathomless depths
the senses of my heart are awake to you.
For fresh soundings of life
for new showings of light
I search in the silence of my spirit, O God.

JOHN PHILIP NEWELL

Face to Face

Day after day, O lord of my life,
shall I stand before thee face to face?
With folded hands, O lord of all worlds,
shall I stand before thee face to face?

Under thy great sky in solitude and silence,
with humble heart shall I stand before thee face to face?

In this laborious world of thine, tumultuous with toil
and with struggle, among hurrying crowds
shall I stand before thee face to face?

And when my work shall be done in this world,
O King of kings, alone and speechless
shall I stand before thee face to face?

TAGORE

The American Indian Ten Commandments

1. The Earth is our Mother; care for Her

2. Honor all your relations.

3. Open your heart and soul to the Great Spirit.

4. All life is sacred; treat all beings with respect.

5. Take from the Earth what is needed and nothing more.

6. Do what needs to be done for the good of all.

7. Give constant thanks to the Great Spirit for each day.

8. Speak the truth but only for the good in others.

9. Follow the rhythms of Nature.

10. Enjoy life's journey; but leave no tracks.

I pray because I can't help myself. I pray because I'm helpless. I pray because the need flows out of me all the time—waking and sleeping. It doesn't change God—it changes me.

C. S. LEWIS

Embodied Prayers to the Trinity

I

Start with hands joined in front of the heart

To God our Father
Inhale and raise arms overhead

To Christ Our Saviour who gave
his life for us on a cross
Exhale arms down into a cruciform T

To the Holy Spirit who dwells within our hearts
Inhale hands over the heart

And within others and all creation
Exhale, extending arms and hands forward

Bring hands back in namaste position over the heart

The second time:

To God our creator
Repeat same movements as above

To Christ our redeemer
To the Holy Spirit the sanctifier
Who dwells in us and in all creation
Bring hands back in namaste position over the heart

The third time, repeat the same movements in silence

II

Strengthen my faith
  Extend arms forward, palms turned up

Deepen our love
  Place one hand on top the other over the heart

Pour out your Holy Spirit upon me
  Goal post arms, hands raised

Stretch forth your hands in signs
and wonders for the sake of your Reign
  Extend arms forward, palms turned down

Teach me how to pray
  Hands together at breast in prayer position

Let me not judge lest I be judged
  Arms folded across chest, head bowed

Grant me a discerning heart
  *Touch hands in prayer position to forehead,
  then to heart*

Help me to live chastely
  Place hands over lower abdomen

Open my hands in service to the needs of others
  Touch feet

III

Stand, with hands joined at the breast

I bow before the Father who made me
> *Bow from the waist, touch fingers of R hand to floor;*
> *rise, making sign of cross holding the first two fingers*
> *and thumb of the R hand together*

I bow before the Son who saved me
> *Repeat above*

I bow before the Spirit who guides me
> *Repeat above*

In love and adoration
> *Join palms of hands six inches from chest*

I give you the affections of my heart
> *Touch thumbs of joined hands to heart*

I give you the words of my mouth
> *Touch joined fingers to lips*

I give you the thoughts of my mind
> *Touch joined fingers to forehead*

I give you the strength of my body
> *Open arms into a wide V and gaze upward*

I bow and adore Thee
> *Down on all fours, touch forehead to floor*

Sacred Three
Turn palms upward, place L foot on top of R

Ever One
Return to table position, curl toes under

The Trinity
Rise to standing, making sign of the cross

THOMAS RYAN, CSP

COURAGE

Courage, we all eventually learn, isn't the absence of fear. It's having the determination to do the right thing in the presence of fear. The greater the danger, the greater the fear; the greater the challenge, the greater our need for courage.

Many men try to avoid the need for courage by playing it safe, by avoiding risk, by taking on only the easiest of challenges. But even those men who try to minimize risks in these ways often find that life won't let them. They may vigorously avoid ten dangers, but then an eleventh comes and takes them by surprise.

Other men have a thirst—we might even say a lust—for adventure. They have a knack for getting themselves into more trouble than they bargained for.

All of these men—and all of us who find ourselves somewhere in between—eventually need to open ourselves up to a courage we have not yet practiced. And that's when prayers like these are so valuable.

Wendell Berry's wise poem sets the stage for the prayers that follow. Being baffled, being impeded ... these are not signs that we have failed—they're signs that we've embarked.

So whether you're traveling into unknown territory, standing up for justice, facing your own inner demons, pondering dangers that your loved ones may face, facing an antagonist, or simply realizing that you've been whining and complaining too much lately, open your heart with these prayers that do not ask for life to be made easier, but ask that we be made stronger.

The Real Work

It may be that when we no longer know what to do
we have come to our real work,

and that when we no longer know which way to go
we have come to our real journey.

The mind that is not baffled is not employed.

The impeded stream is the one that sings.

WENDELL BERRY

The Merton Prayer

MY LORD GOD, I have no idea where I am going. I do not see the road ahead of me. I cannot know for certain where it will end. Nor do I really know myself, and the fact that I think I am following your will does not mean that I am actually doing so. But I believe that the desire to please you does in fact please you. And I hope I have that desire in all that I am doing. I hope that I will never do anything apart from that desire. And I know that if I do this you will lead me by the right road, though I may know nothing about it. Therefore I will trust you always though I may seem to be lost and in the shadow of death. I will not fear, for you are ever with me, and you will never leave me to face my perils alone.

THOMAS MERTON

Prayer to the Great Spirit

Great Spirit hear my call
and teach me of these things
I do not know
let me walk free with the wolf clan
so I may learn their wisdom
through the eyes of our sacred
of your creation
Give me strength to protect and preserve
what we have left of our Mother Earth
make me wise to teach others to follow
the path meant for us to take
by your grace
in this world now out of place
from our human race
I am only but one man
but guide me to help save
what we have taken away
with our ignorance and destruction
bring peace and harmony back again
for many generations to come
to end this misery of pain
so our children will live a life they deserve
Let me bring light into the hearts
of the shallow
and show them the ways of long ago

to walk in footprints of my ancestors
that for many years have softly tread
on the beauty of this precious land
Let these river's run wide and freely flow
with the presence of every touch by your hand
bring back what was for so long dead
let this sun shine on this sacred ground
that is covered in blood flowing red
with our hate and greed
Heal these wounds I bleed
make me a warrior a chosen one
to forever stand proud and tall
when times are hard and tears fall
from what we have done
Show me the way when my people forget
our true purpose and meaning here
so that I may bring better days tomorrow
of yesterdays forever gone
in these times of sorrow
one day we will all soon regret
Let me not walk in fear
in this moment of need
as I ask of your guidance on my vision
and my journey
you had given to me

SPIRITWIND WOOD

Prayers and Thanksgivings, "For Guidance"

Direct us, O Lord, in all our doings with your most gracious favor, and further us with your continual help; that in all our works begun, continued, and ended in you, we may glorify your holy Name, and finally, by your mercy, obtain everlasting life; through Jesus Christ our Lord.

Amen.

BOOK OF COMMON PRAYER

[To have Faith in Christ] means, of course, trying to do all that He says. There would be no sense in saying you trusted a person if you would not take his advice. Thus if you have really handed yourself over to Him, it must follow that you are trying to obey Him. But trying in a new way, a less worried way. Not doing these things in order to be saved, but because He has begun to save you already. Not hoping to get to Heaven as a reward for your actions, but inevitably wanting to act in a certain way because a first faint gleam of Heaven is already inside you.

C. S. LEWIS

That night I addressed a meeting of African township ministers in Cape Town. I mention this because the opening prayer of one of the ministers has stayed with me over these many years and was a source of strength at a difficult time. He thanked the Lord for His bounty and goodness, for His mercy and His concern for all men. But then he took the liberty of reminding the Lord that some of His subjects were more downtrodden than others, and that it sometimes seemed as though He was not paying attention. The minister then said that if the Lord did not show a little more initiative in leading the black man to salvation, the black man would have to take matters in his own two hands.

Amen.

NELSON MANDELA

Faith Poem

I need no assurances—I am a man who is
    preoccupied of his own soul;
I do not doubt that whatever I know at a given time,
    there waits for me more which I do not know;
I do not doubt that from under the feet, and beside
    the hands and face I am cognizant of, are now
    looking faces I am not cognizant of—calm and
    actual faces;
I do not doubt but the majesty and beauty of the
    world is latent in any iota of the world;
I do not doubt there are realizations I have no idea
    of, waiting for me through time and through the
    universes—also upon this earth;
I do not doubt I am limitless, and that the universes
    are limitless—in vain I try to think how limitless;
I do not doubt that the orbs, and the systems of
    orbs, play their swift sports through the air on
    purpose—and that I shall one day be eligible to
    do as much as they, and more than they;
I do not doubt there is far more in trivialities,
    insects, vulgar persons, slaves, dwarfs, weeds,
    rejected refuse, than I have supposed;
I do not doubt there is more in myself than I
    have supposed—and more in all men and

women— and more in my poems than I have
supposed;

I do not doubt that temporary affairs keep on and
on, millions of years;

I do not doubt interiors have their interiors, and
exteriors have their exteriors—and that the
eye-sight has another eye-sight, and the hearing
another hearing, and the voice another voice;

I do not doubt that the passionately-wept deaths
of young men are provided for—and that the
deaths of young women, and the deaths of little
children, are provided for;

I do not doubt that wrecks at sea, no matter what
the horrors of them—no matter whose wife,
child, husband, father, lover, has gone down—
are provided for, to the minutest point;

I do not doubt that shallowness, meanness,
malignance, are provided for;

I do not doubt that cities, you, America, the
remainder of the earth, politics, freedom,
degradations, are carefully provided for;

I do not doubt that whatever can possibly happen,
any where, at any time, is provided for, in the
inherences of things.

WALT WHITMAN

The Traveler's Prayer

May it be Your will, Eternal One, our God and the God of our ancestors, that You lead us toward peace, emplace our footsteps towards peace, guide us toward peace, and make us reach our desired destination for life, gladness, and peace. May You rescue us from the hand of every foe, ambush, bandits and wild animals along the way, and from all manner of punishments that assemble to come to Earth. May You send blessing in our every handiwork, and grant us peace, kindness, and mercy in your eyes and in the eyes of all who see us. May You hear the sound of our supplication, because You are the God who hears prayer and supplications. Blessed are You, Eternal One, who hears prayer.

A Father's Prayer for Loved Ones

Kind Father, I thank You for my home where
  loved ones dwell
and to which my fondest memories now turn.
I praise You for the family love and peace and cheer
which follow me and comfort me in strange and
  distant places.
I am grateful for all things we share in common,
the worthy lessons we learn,
the hardships and griefs we sometimes bear,
the tasks and pleasures which bind us closer to
  each other,
and the abiding affection and heartfelt prayers
which still keep our spirits one in You.
Shelter my home, O God,
and all my dear ones there.
Make me strong, unselfish,
and brave to defend and protect them.
Send down Your peace to every family on earth
and grant an abundance of grace to them
so that in doing Your will
they may merit the joys of eternal salvation.

Amen.

A Usual Prayer

According to Thy will: That this day only
I may avoid the vile
and baritone away in a broader chorus
of to each other decent forebearance & even aid.

Merely sensational let's have today,
lacking mostly thinking—
men's thinking being eighteen-tenths deluded.
Did I get this figure out of St Isaac of Syria?

For fun: find me among my self-indulgent artbooks
a new drawing by Ingres!
For discipline, two self-denying minus-strokes
and my wonted isometrics, barbells, & antiphons.

Lord of happenings, & little things,
muster me westward fitter to my end—
which has got to be Your strange end for me—
and toughen me effective to the tribes en route.

JOHN BERRYMAN

Hashem:

Grant me the ability to be alone!

May it be my custom to go outdoors each day
   among the trees and grass—
among all growing things,
and there may I be alone,
and enter into prayer,
to talk with the One to whom I belong.
May I express there everything in my heart,
and may all the foliage of the field—
all grasses, trees and plants—
awake at my coming,
to send the powers of their life into the words of
   my prayer
so that my prayer and speech are made whole
through the life and the spirit of all growing things,
which are made as one by their transcendent Source.
May I then pour out the words of my heart
before your Presence like water, Hashem,
and lift up my hands to You in song,
on my behalf, and that of my children!

   REBBE NACHMAN OF BRESLOV

Grit Seasoning

While I do this grit
work, season
the irksome pieces
with enough
Ahas! to remind me
of the reason.

KENT IRA GROFF

A man only begins to be a man when he ceases to whine and revile, and commences to search for the hidden justice which regulates his life. And he adapts his mind to that regulating factor, he ceases to accuse others as the cause of his condition, and builds himself up in strong and noble thoughts; ceases to kick against circumstances, but begins to use them as aids to his more rapid progress, and as a means of the hidden powers and possibilities within himself.

JAMES ALLEN

For the Lost

Brother.
I am not your rival.
I am not your enemy.
I am not the source of
Your fear and shame,
Your grief and loss,
Your loneliness
Or your nightmares.
I am your fellow.
Lost, at times, like you,
But never alone.
I rise above these struggles toward
A vision of my best self.

This is my work and my prayer:
Come with me as companion and friend,
And I will come with you as a gift of love,
Seeing you,
Holding your life as sacred,
Your journey as an adventure,
Your wisdom as a gift.

Drop your weapon and remove your mask
So that you can see truth.
For, in truth, your mask is neither power nor shelter.

It is thin as air,
Clear as glass,
Transparent, fragile, useless.

I see you, brother.
See me.
See this man.
Your right arm.
Your staff.
Your comfort.
Welcome home.

ALDEN SOLOVY

He who finds fault with others is himself in the
wrong.
With earnest, tread the path and see not the
mistakes of the world.

THE SUTRA OF HUI NENG

To Bless the Space between Us

I bless the night that nourished my heart
To set the ghosts of longing free
Into the flow and figure of dream
That went to harvest from the dark
Bread for the hunger no one sees.

All that is eternal in me
Welcomes the wonder of this day,
The field of brightness it creates
Offering time for each thing
To arise and illuminate.

I place on the altar of dawn:
The quiet loyalty of breath,
The tent of thought where I shelter,
Waves of desire I am shore to
And all beauty drawn to the eye.

May my mind come alive today
To the invisible geography
That invites me to new frontiers,
To break the dead shell of yesterdays,
To risk being disturbed and changed.

May I have the courage today
To live the life that I would love,

To postpone my dream no longer
But do at last what I came here for
And waste my heart on fear no more.

JOHN O'DONOHUE

Exploring the Inner Sanctuary

1. Wherever you are, sit comfortably and close your eyes. Take several slow, deep breaths. If any thoughts beg for attention, release them. As thoughts continue to spring up, don't give them any attention, and they will find their own way out.

2. Wait patiently. Listen expectantly. Hear the sound of nothing—it is amazing how overwhelming silence can be. It possesses a roar of its own.

3. When you are able to spend fifteen minutes in silence without feeling that you should be doing something else, begin to look inward. Pay attention to the rhythm of your breath.

4. Notice other sensations in your body. Imagine that with each inhalation the breath of God enters you. Feel the tingle of exhilaration as you become aware that God is within you.

5. If you are one who benefits from visualization, allow your mind's eye to visualize your waiting for God, being open to God's manifestation.

6. When you become aware of God's presence, sit quietly with it. Enjoy the moments.

7. If it feels permissible to do so, offer words of praise or ask questions that are relevant to your current situation.

8. Continue to wait quietly. Listen for the response of your Inner Witness.

9. Be attentive to sensations and impressions that well up within you. What images or thoughts come to mind? What feelings can you identify?

10. Tend to those sensations and impressions. What can you learn from them? How might they guide you?

11. If a feeling of gratitude and thankfulness emerges as a response to the presence of the Other, express it to that presence, or to those who enrich your life.

JAY MARSHALL

HEALING

There's a lot wrong with this world, and some of it is our fault. When that's the case, good men learn to ask for forgiveness.

There's a lot in this world that has been broken, and sometimes we've seen others do the breaking. When that's the case, the world needs men who seek the grace to forgive.

There's a lot in this world that is wounded, which is why the world needs men who become channels of healing power, healing love, healing wisdom, healing presence.

There's a lot in each of us that is worn out or worn down or ticked off or drained dry or otherwise messed up. If we don't process our pain, we'll pass it on, which will only make things worse for us. And not only that, but then we'll make things worse for others. So the world needs good men who learn—through prayer—to process their pain.

Life's wounds will cause us either to break down or break through, to become bitter—or better. Here are prayers to help men like you and me resist the bitterness and choose the betterness—because there's a lot wrong with the world.

We have come to heal wounds, to bind up the brokenhearted and to bring home those who have lost their way.

Attributed to **ST. FRANCIS OF ASSISI**

Imagine yourself as a living house. God comes in to rebuild that house. At first, perhaps, you can understand what He is doing. He is getting the drains right and stopping the leaks in the roof and so on; you knew that those jobs needed doing and so you are not surprised. But presently He starts knocking the house about in a way that hurts abominably and does not seem to make any sense. What on earth is He up to? The explanation is that He is building quite a different house from the one you thought of—throwing out a new wing here, putting on an extra floor there, running up towers, making courtyards. You thought you were being made into a decent little cottage: but He is building a palace. He intends to come and live in it Himself.

C. S. LEWIS

Expand My Heart

Expand my heart, Jesus.
Pull it and stretch it
to make there a shelter
for the widow and the orphan,
for the sick friend or colleague.

Let not your broken, naked
body on the cross ever become
for me a visual cliché.
Let it rather be a riveting icon
of a heart pierced and drained
to heal and make us whole,
of hands and feet nailed down
to set us free from our captivities,
of a head hanging limp in death
so that we might look up with hope in life.

Make me, Jesus, a great lover
in the small things of daily living,
attentive to a child's need
or an old person's limitation;
responsive to a loved one's joy
or a neighbor's grief.

Soak, wash, rinse, shake
and hang out this heart of mine
to blow in the wind of your Spirit
until it be easily folded in love.
Reduce me, Lord, to love.

THOMAS RYAN, CSP

What has anyone done to deserve your grace?
  Lord, do I really have any cause to complain
  or lash out at you when I do not get what I
  want? Surely, Lord, I am nothing. I can do
  nothing. I am not capable of any good on my
  own. I am broken and inclined to unhealthy,
  self-destructive choices. Unless you help and
  inwardly instruct me, I become altogether cold
  and distant from you....

Only you can help me, without the aid of any
  other, and strengthen my heart and mind so as
  to rest in you alone, resolute, unchanging, and
  secure.

O my truth, my mercy, my God, most blessed
  Trinity, to you alone be praise, honor, power,
  and glory for evermore.

  THOMAS À KEMPIS

A Passing-On Prayer

When the sunset of this miraculous life arrives
and its twilight shadows fade away,
while dreams of the next begin to dawn
and appear more vividly before the eyes
    of your noble consciousness;

May the inner-light essence
    of the Buddha
and all the radiant awakened ones
continuously guide you
    onwards and upwards
on the evolutionary path of spiritual enlightenment.

adapted from Tibetan sources by LAMA SŪRYA DĀS

Ah! from how great bitterness of soul have you often delivered me, O Good Jesus, coming to me!... How often has prayer taken me on the brink of despair, and restored me to the state of soul of one exulting in joy and confident forgiveness. Those who are afflicted in this way, behold they know that the Lord Jesus is truly a Physician Who healeth the broken of heart and bindeth up their bruises.

BERNARD OF CLAIRVAUX

Leaving

A leaf that has served its function
as a thing of beauty
can only become
nurturing
humus
when it
leaves:
detaching
as it grieves,
it fails and falls
to the Ground of its being
to nurture another thing of beauty.

KENT IRA GROFF

Prayer for Tolerance

O Thou God of all beings, of all worlds, and of
   all times,
We pray, that the little differences in our clothes,
In our inadequate languages,
In our ridiculous customs,
In our imperfect laws,
In our illogical opinions,
In our ranks and conditions which are so
   disproportionately important to us
And so meaningless to you,
That these small variations
That distinguish those atoms that we call men,
   one from another,
May not be signals of hatred and persecution!

   VOLTAIRE

Holding Hands

Oh, Lord of the Dance,
Four weeks ago
we slow-danced in the kitchen,
I bore most of her weight, but we smiled
as the music reminded us of our first date.
Two weeks ago
she was too weak to get out of bed,
seldom able to speak.
I stayed with her, holding her hand, speaking softly.
I often hummed her favorite tune—
the one to which we danced.
Four days ago
she slipped away.
I was still holding her hand.
Today, Lord,
I need you to hold my hand and my heart.
Both are shaky now—
I need your steady hand and loving heart—
I need you to bear most of my weight in this new dance.

DR. BENJAMIN PRATT

A fool is happy
Until his mischief turns against him.

And a good man may suffer
Until his goodness flowers.

DHAMMAPADA

O little self, within whose smallness lies
All that man was, and is, and will become,
Atom unseen that comprehends the skies
And tells the tracks by which the planets roam.
That, without moving, knows the joys of wings,
The tiger's strength, the eagle's secrecy,
And in the hovel can consort with kings,
Or clothe a god with his own mystery.
O with what darkness do we cloak thy light,
What dusty folly gather thee for food,
Thou who alone art knowledge and delight,
The heavenly bread, the beautiful, the good.
O living self, O god, O morning star,
Give us thy light, forgive us what we are.

JOHN MASEFIELD, OM

Anima Christi, Soul of Christ

Soul of Christ, sanctify me.
Body of Christ, save me.
Blood of Christ, inebriate me.
Water from the side of Christ, wash me.
Passion of Christ, strengthen me.
O Good Jesus, hear me.
Within Thy wounds hide me.
Suffer me not to be separated from thee.
From the malignant enemy defend me.
In the hour of my death call me.
And bid me come unto Thee,
That with all Thy saints,
I may praise thee
Forever and ever.
Amen.

Attributed to ST. IGNATIUS LOYOLA

I'm impatient, Lord,
and it drives me crazy,
to say nothing of those around me.
But you don't seem to have deadlines, God.
Who would set them, after all?
You have eternity.
I don't!

So, forgive me, I want quick miracles,
quick miracles of healing,
of reconciling, of changing for good.
of justice rolling down now,
and of peace coming to the world, to my heart,
of water turning into wine,
grief and joy turning into joy
within at most a season's breath.

Quick miracles, Lord, not slow ones,
which are your specialty, it seems
so slow people die in the meantime,
and children starve, are shot,
storms and droughts destroy,
hate and indifference flourish,
cruelty rules the day,
my life slips away.

Life is short!
I have deadlines!

I am not a patient person.
I have only so much time to strive,
to accomplish what I gave to do,
to right some wrongs, to make amends,
to create some beauty, help the poor,
welcome the outcast gays,
clear the ghettos, repair the city,
only so much time—I'm not God, you know.

Maybe that's the dis-ease
for which impatience is the symptom,
I'm not God and I forget it
act compulsively as though I know
what needs doing and when,
as though I am you.
a faithless confusion,
I realize.
But, damn it, God, I don't have eternity.
Or do I?

I suppose that's really what this prayer
comes up to:
Do I have eternity?
To be convinced a little that I do,

that you do have it with me, for me,
would be miracle enough, I do believe,
for then I would likely be a more patient man,
and that, says Paul,
is the first degree of love,
and the world and I both
could use a great
many more degrees of that.

So, God, this is what I ask,
that you would pull off in me
this one miracle quick enough
to finish in my short remaining years.
Perhaps you've begun, I hope,
by giving me pause to rest in this prayer,
which is to rest in you.
Thank you.

Amen.

TED LODER

The Rain Has Held Back for Days

The rain has held back for days and days,
my God, in my arid heart.
The horizon is fiercely naked—
not the thinnest cover of a soft cloud,
not the vaguest hint of a distant cool shower.
Send thy angry storm, dark with death,
if it is thy wish, and with lashes of lightning
startle the sky from end to end.
But call back, my lord,
call back this pervading silent heat,
still and keen and cruel,
burning the heart with dire despair.
Let the cloud of grace bend low from above
like the tearful look of the mother on the day of
    the father's wrath.

TAGORE

For since the beginning of the world
Men have not heard nor perceived by the ear,
Nor has the eye seen any God besides You,
Who acts for the one who waits for Him.

You meet him who rejoices and does
    righteousness,
Who remembers You in Your ways.
You are indeed angry, for we have sinned—
In these ways we continue; and we need to be
    saved.

But we are all like an unclean thing,
And all our righteousnesses are like filthy rags;
We all fade as a leaf,
And our iniquities, like the wind, have taken us
    away.

And there is no one who calls on Your name,
Who stirs himself up to take hold of You;
For You have hidden Your face from us,
And have consumed us because of our iniquities.

But now, O Lord, You are our Father;
We are the clay, and You our potter;
And all we are the work of Your hand.

Do not be furious, O Lord,
Nor remember iniquity forever;
Indeed, Please look—We all are Your people!

ISAIAH 64:4–9

Miracles

Were I God almighty, I would ordain,
rain fall lightly where old men trod,
no death in childbirth, neither infant nor mother,
ditches firm fenced against the errant blind,
aircraft come to ground like any feather.

No mischance, malice, knives.
Tears dried. Would resolve all
flaw and blockage of mind
that makes us mad, sets lives awry.

So I pray, under
the sign of the world's murder, the ruined son;
why are you silent?
feverish as lions
hear us in the world,
caged, devoid of hope.

Still, some redress and healing.
The hand of an old woman
turns gospel page;
it flares up gently, the sudden tears of Christ.

DANIEL BERRIGAN

The Serenity Prayer

God, grant me the serenity to accept the things I
   cannot change,
Courage to change the things I can,
And wisdom to know the difference.

Light Beams

Great Spirit:
hold us all ways in your sway,
help us ever more to stay
in your rays of light,
in your gaze at night,
in your ways of right.

Let your fiery rays converge
and merge to set ablaze
the tender tinder of our hearts,
and there ignite a living flame of love
that shall surely guide us
better than a known way:
that shall surely guide us
better than a known way,
better than a known way,
better than a known way.

KENT IRA GROFF

A Prayer for Parenting

Parent of All:
You have blessed us with children,
> with the *b'rit*/covenant of parenthood,
> with deep reservoirs of love, concern,
> responsibility, and guidance.

Thank You, Close One,
> for the astounding privilege of parenting;
> for discovering capacities we had not known in
> ourselves;
> for the blessings of health, safety, discovery, joy,
>> and love for, and from, our children and
>> all children;
> for opening our minds with curiosity,
>> our hearts with compassion,
>>> our communities with care.

Help us to emulate the care of your *Shekhinah*:
> To listen well and to respond sensitively;
> To be open and flexible, or clear and unyielding,
> as necessary;
> To maintain boundaries and yet to extend
> ourselves in some new ways;
> To know when to speak and when to be silent;

To speak truth and match our deeds to our
words;
To rely on profound beliefs and hard-earned
knowledge,
but also to be able to take risks if required;
To have faith in ourselves and in our world
so that we can do what is needed;
To maintain hope and vision when the challenges
before us are so hard.

When we are wracked by worry,
Help us reach for calm and equilibrium.
When we find ourselves confused and lost,
Open for us Your Torah and the Torah of
loving parents' lived experience.
When disappointment, frustration, or rage mount
within us,
Enable us to keep perspective, consider different
options,
and channel the energy towards
relationship and renewal.

Help us, Parent of all parents, to care for ourselves
properly and regularly,
in body, mind, and spirit,
so that we can be as present and effective
as possible,

and model the *shmirat hanefesh*/self care we
want our children to emulate.

May the words of Your prophet Malachi be fulfilled:
"Behold, I will send you Elijah
the prophet
before the coming of the great and terrible
day of Adonai:
And he shall turn the heart of the parents
to the children,
and the heart of the children to
their parents."

Amen.

RABBI SIMKHA Y. WEINTRAUB

Deep peace of the running wave to you.
Deep peace of the flowing air to you.
Deep peace of the quiet earth to you.
Deep peace of the shining stars to you.
Deep peace of the infinite peace to you.

CELTIC PRAYER

Centering Prayer

The following guidelines for practice come from Father Thomas Keating, who taught me the art of Centering Prayer.

1. Choose a sacred word as an expression of your intention to know the will of God. This word can be anything that sets the right intention. You may choose a name of God, such as Jesus, Allah, Krishna, Adonai, or something less "holy," such as "Yes," "Love," "Peace," "Shalom," or "Salaam." What makes a word sacred in the context of Centering Prayer is that it holds your intention to be present.

2. Sit comfortably with your eyes closed. Take a moment to settle down. Allow your breathing to quiet as your body becomes still. Then introduce your sacred word, repeating it over and over, perhaps in sync with your breathing but perhaps not. As you do so, you are consenting over and again to the will of God.

3. If your mind wanders from your sacred word, gently return your attention to it. Distracting thoughts, feelings, physical sensations are natural to Centering Prayer. They are not your enemy. On the contrary, every distraction is an opportunity for kenosis, selfemptying. By returning to your sacred word you are letting go of distractions, and by letting go of

distractions you are emptying yourself of the self that feeds on them.

4. When the allotted time for Centering Prayer is over, allow yourself two more minutes to simply sit in the silence with your eyes closed. If you so choose, you can formally bring your Centering Prayer time to a close with a vocalized prayer or poem or some gesture of thanksgiving.

RAMI SHAPIRO

STRENGTH

There is a kind of masculine strength that is characterized by brashness, brazenness, boast, and bravado, which are sure and certain signs that the man in question is not a man of prayer. Prayer breeds a different kind of strength in men and the prayers in this section help you see that strength so you too can aspire to it—and ask for it and receive it.

You'll see this deeper, wiser, more mature strength in a prayer taken from the Book of Common Prayer. It associates quiet confidence and stillness with strength.

You'll see it in another prayer in this section that seeks humility, the ability to listen, and wonder. How different from the false strength that pridefully exaggerates how much it knows and that speaks in certain declarations devoid of wonder.

You'll see it in a father's prayer for his son that does not ask for riches, fame, comfort, power, or ease, but seeks strength in better things.

You'll see it in a moving Sioux prayer that begins its search for strength with the words, "I am small and weak."

You'll see it in a prayer from Hindu poet Tagore, who associates strength not with conquest but with surrender.

What a tragedy—for a man to succeed in being strong, but in so doing, to have sought a foolish kind of strength. Prayers like these challenge me to walk a better way ... in the words of the Cherokee prayer from this section, to "walk like a man."

Cherokee Prayer

As I walk the trail of life
in the fear of the wind and rain,
grant O Great Spirit
that I may always walk
like a man.

AUTHOR UNKNOWN

To George and Georgiana Keats ("The Vale of Soul-Making")

To George and Georgiana Keats

Sunday Morn, Feb. 14th, 1819

My Dear Brother & Sister—

Even here though I myself am pursueing the same instinctive course as the veriest human animal you can think of—I am however young writing at random—straining at particles of light in the midst of a great darkness—without knowing the bearing of any one assertion of any one opinion. Yet may I not in this be free from sin? May there not be superior beings amused with any graceful, though instinctive attitude my mind may fall into, as I am entertained with the alertness of a Stoat or the anxiety of a Deer? Though a quarrel in the Streets is a thing to be bated, the energies displayed in it are fine; the commonest Man shows a grace in his quarrel—By a superior being our reasonings may take the same tone— though erroneous they may be fine—This is the very thing in which consists poetry; and if so it is not so fine a thing as philosophy—For the same reason that an eagle is not so fine a thing as a truth—Give me this credit—Do you not think I strive to know myself?

JOHN KEATS

Lead Kindly Light

Lead, Kindly Light, amid the encircling gloom,
Lead me Thou on! The night is dark, and I am
far from home, Lead Thou me on! Keep Thou
my feet; I do not ask to see the distant scene; one
step is enough for me. I was not ever thus, nor
pray'd that Thou shouldst lead me on; I loved
to choose and see my path, but now lead Thou
me on! I loved the garish day, and, spite of fears,
pride ruled my will: remember not past years.
So long Your power hath blest me, sure it still
will lead me on, o'er moor and fen, o'er crag and
torrent, till the night is gone; and with the morn
those angel faces smile which I have loved long
since, and lost awhile.

JOHN HENRY NEWMAN

O God of peace, who has taught us that in returning and rest we shall be saved, in quietness and confidence shall be our strength: By the might of your Spirit lift us, we pray to your presence, where we may be still and know that you are God; through Jesus Christ our Lord.

Amen.

BOOK OF COMMON PRAYER

It suffices me for attaining to all righteousness, to have Him alone propitious toward me against whom alone I have sinned.... Not to sin is the righteousness of God: Man's righteousness is God's forgiveness.

BERNARD OF CLAIRVAUX

A Father's Day Prayer

Let us praise those fathers who by their own account were not always there for their children, but who continue to offer those children, now grown, their love and support.

Let us pray for those fathers who have been wounded by the neglect and hostility of their children.

Let us praise those fathers who, despite divorce, have remained in their children's lives.

Let us praise those fathers whose children are adopted, and whose love and support has offered healing.

Let us praise those fathers who, as stepfathers, freely choose the obligation of fatherhood and earned their stepchildren's love and respect.

Let us praise those fathers who have lost a child to death, and continue to hold the child in their heart.

Let us praise those men who have no children, but cherish the next generation as if they were their own.

Let us praise those men who have "fathered" us in their role as mentors and guides.

Let us praise those men who are about to become fathers; may they openly delight in their children.

And let us praise those fathers who have died, but live on in our memory and whose love continues to nurture us.

KIRK LOADMAN-COPELAND

As a man thinketh in his heart, so shall he be.

JAMES ALLEN

Help Me Listen

O Holy One
I hear and say so many words,
yet yours is the word I need.
Speak now,
and help me listen
and, if what I hear is silence,
let it quiet me,
let it disturb me,
let it touch my need,
let it break my pride,
let it shrink my certainties,
let it enlarge my wonder.

TED LODER

A Father's Prayer

Build me a son, O Lord,
who will be strong enough to know when he is weak,
and brave enough to face himself when he is afraid;
one who will be proud and unbending in honest defeat,
and humble and gentle in victory.

Lead him, I pray,
not in the path of ease and comfort,
but under the stress and spur of difficulties and
    challenge.

Here let him learn to stand up in the storm;
here let him learn compassion for those who fail.

Build me a son whose heart will be clear,
whose goal will be high,
a son who will master himself
before he seeks to master other men,
one who will reach into the future,
yet never forget the past.

And, after all these things are his,
give him, I pray,
enough of a sense of humor,
so that he may always be serious,
yet never take himself too seriously.

Give him humility,
so that he may always remember the simplicity of
    true greatness,
the open mind of true strength.
Then I, his father,
will dare to whisper,
'I have not lived in vain.'

    GENERAL DOUGLAS MACARTHUR

My Strength and my Song;
Who was, is, and will be my Salvation.

PSALM 118:14

I have never gone to sleep with a grievance
   against anyone.
And, as far as I could, I have never let anyone go
   to sleep with a grievance against me.

ABBA AGATHON

May I be among those who are hard to provoke
and easy to appease.

May I be a friend of peace at home and at work,
and everywhere I go.

When I am angry let me reflect whether my anger
is proportionate to its cause and appropriate in
its expression.

May I strive at all times to keep from adding to
the world's woes.

RABBI CHAIM STERN

Wrestle Me Now, Lord!

Lord, I need you to be rougher with me.
I have gotten too proud, too successful, too
  brazen, too full of myself!
I beg you to come in the night,
as you did with Jacob,
and wrestle me,
push my face into a mirror
until my heart screams "Uncle,"
until my soul will face my demons,
those temptations that have led me far into the
  wilderness.
I hope you don't have to break my hip;
I hope you will wrestle me
to become a better self.
Come, Lord, do come,
Take me down a notch or two!

DR. BENJAMIN PRATT

I will be with him in trouble; I will deliver him and honour him.

PSALM 91:15

First, "I will deliver." When God called Moses
to go down into Egypt to deliver the children of
Israel from the hand of the Egyptians, in all the
world there wasn't a man who, humanly speaking,
was less qualified than Moses. He had made the
attempt once before to deliver the children of
Israel, and he began by delivering one man. He
failed in that, and killed an Egyptian, and had
to run off into the desert, and stay there forty
years. He had tried to deliver the Hebrews in his
own way, he was working in his own strength
and doing it in the energy of the flesh. He had
all the wisdom of the Egyptians, but that didn't
help him. He had to be taken back into Horeb,
and kept there forty years in the school of
God, before God could trust him to deliver the
children of Israel in God's way. Then God came
to him and said, "I have come down to deliver,"
and when God worked through Moses three
million were delivered as easy as I can turn my
hand over. God could do it. It was no trouble
when God came on the scene.

Learn the lesson. If we want to be delivered, from every inward and outward foe, we must look to a higher source than ourselves. We cannot do it in our own strength.

D. L. MOODY

A Sioux Prayer

O, Great Spirit,
whose voice I hear in the winds
and whose breath gives life to all the world, hear me.
I am small and weak.
I need your strength and wisdom.
Let me walk in beauty and make my eyes
ever behold the red and purple sunset.
Make my hands respect the things you have made
and my ears sharp to hear your voice.
Make me wise so that I may understand
the things you have taught my people.
Let me learn the lessons you have hidden
in every leaf and rock.
I seek strength, not to be superior to my brother,
but to fight my greatest enemy—myself.
Make me always ready to come to you
with clean hands and straight eyes,
so when life fades, as the fading sunset,
my spirit will come to you
without shame.

CHIEF YELLOW LARK

To her who gives and takes back all, to nature ...
give what you will, take back what you will.

MARCUS AURELIUS

Generosity cultivates life, strength, beauty, wit and ease.
The giver participates in each of these qualities, both in heaven and among men.

ANGUTTARA NIKAYA

My Prayer

This is my prayer to thee, my lord—strike,
strike at the root of penury in my heart.
Give me the strength lightly to bear my joys and
sorrows.
Give me the strength to make my love fruitful in
service.
Give me the strength never to disown the poor or
bend my knees before insolent might.
Give me the strength to raise my mind high
above daily trifles.
And give me the strength to surrender my
strength to thy will with love.

TAGORE

The Three-Minute Breathing Space

Bring your body into an upright and dignified sitting position, with both feet on the floor.

First, listen to sounds. How many different sounds can you hear? As best you can, allow the sounds to be just the way they are.

After a minute, be aware of sensations in your hands. Feel your hands from the inside. Again, allow these sensations to be just the way they are.

Then shift your attention to your breathing. Notice where you feel your breath most prominently in your body: whether at your nostrils, your rib cage, or your abdomen. Station your attention at that place. Feel the physical sensations of your breath as it moves in and out of that spot.

Finally, see if you can be aware of all three at once, like three notes in a musical chord: sounds, sensations in your hands, and the in-out of your breathing.

Do this for three minutes.

As you breathe in, imagine inflating a balloon in your belly. As you breathe out, let the breath release from your body on its own, without forcing or pushing it out. Just let go.

GORDON PEERMAN

HOPE

My faculty advisor in graduate school was a character, especially when drunk, which seemed to happen at every after-hours departmental gathering. I remember at one such gathering—a "holiday festivity," as I recall it being named—I needed to ask him a question about graduation requirements or some such thing. I found him near the drink table, as expected. He answered my question somewhat unhelpfully and then, empty glass in hand, looked me straight in the eye.

"Young man," he slurred—he probably had forgotten my name for the fourth or fifth time—"I want to tell you something, something nobody else will ever tell you."

"Uh, OK," I said, sitting down next to him.

"Young and innocent man, you have no way to have intellectually or existentially assimy- ... assimilated this hidden gnosis because of the paw ... paucity of your years and the relative vacuity of your life exp ... exper ... experience. But I, as your advisor, will advise you."

He smiled a goofy smile and cocked his head in a less-than-sober way, and raised his glass, as if giving me a toast. I didn't have a drink, so I simply nodded, not knowing what else to do.

"I am fully one hundred percent certain that you have on multiple occasions been informed that life is short and that you should grab for all the gusto you can, carpe diem and all that crock of ... poppycock. But this is pure prevarication. The truth ..."—now he leaned forward so I could take in the full aroma of his chemically-enhanced breath—"... and I mean that with a capital T, the Capital-T Truth is that life is long and you had better be prepared for that. Life is long, young man, especially in the middle. Believe me, I know."

The poor man slurred on and on, and I patiently listened until another faculty member came by and rescued me from his impromptu lecture. "Ah," she whispered in my ear, "he's playing Polonius again. He does that whenever he drinks Scotch. It turns him into a surreal cross between Franz Kafka and Walt Whitman—odd and pompous." (Did I mention I was an English major?)

Here I am, over thirty years later, a little past the middle of middle age, about the age of my inebriated professor, come to think of it, and I now realize what he meant. Yes, life is short, as they say. The days fly by. But it is also long. There are a lot of days in rapid succession, and they can easily be misspent or wasted ... one at a time. With so many days, great losses can be accumulated. And we had indeed better be prepared for that.

To have a long life means that if one is headed in a certain direction, one will go a long way on that path. If it's a good direction, wonderful—we will be ever moving higher up and deeper in. But if we lose our way, even a small divergence over time can take us far afield from where we hoped to be. Life is indeed long.

And that's another reason men should pray. Over the course of a long life, prayer helps us stay the course. If faith is a sail to catch the wind, hope is a keel to stay the course. Hope gives us a reference point in the future so that we don't wander aimlessly through life, turning our middle into a muddle. Hope helps us wait well, whether we're waiting in unfulfillment, waiting in pain, waiting in sadness, waiting in bafflement, maybe waiting in boredom.

The prayers in this section can help us cope with the long middle of life. They can help us wait well. As I've read and reread them, I've been struck by words like *when, end, season, first, finally, always, future, before, after, forever, sustain, maintain, persevere*: time words.

Prayers like these help us live well over time, so we begin well, continue well, and in the end, end well, too.

Then, I think, we will feel more that life has been short, and we will have a thirst for more, which will elicit from us a special kind of hope, hope that dares to look beyond and above and below death for meaning that transcends time. And that is a kind of hope that can only be developed over time, through prayers like these.

Love Is Everything

In the way of God *thoughts* count for little, *love* is
    everything.
Nor is it needful ... that we should have great
    things to do.... We can do *little* things for God;
I turn the cake that is frying on the pan for the
    love of Him....

BROTHER LAWRENCE

Do not dwell upon the sins and mistakes of yesterday so exclusively as to have no energy and mind left for living rightly today, and do not think that the sins of yesterday can prevent you from living purely today.

JAMES ALLEN

May He support us all the day long, till the shades lengthen, and the evening comes, and the busy world is hushed, and the fever of life is over, and our work is done! Then in His mercy may He give us safe lodging, and a holy rest, and peace at the last!

JOHN HENRY NEWMAN

Time and No-Time

Time is endless in thy hands, my lord.
There is none to count thy minutes.

Days and nights pass and ages bloom and fade
    like flowers.
Thou knowest how to wait.

Thy centuries follow each other perfecting a
    small wildflower.

We have no time to lose,
and having no time we must scramble for our
    chances.
We are too poor to be late.

And thus it is that time goes by
while I give it to every querulous man who claims it,
and thine altar is empty of all offerings to the last.

At the end of the day I hasten in fear lest thy gate
    be shut;
but I find that yet there is time.

TAGORE

Blessing of a Father

Lord Jesus, our brother,
we praise You for saving us.
Teach us to love you and Your Father
by keeping Your commandments.

Bless + this father,
and deepen his love for his wife and family.
By his work and example and prayer,
may he lead his children to follow You.

Lord Jesus,
hear our prayer as we offer You glory
for ever and ever.

Amen.

Follow My Ways and I Will Lead You

Follow my ways and I will lead you
To golden-haired suns,
Logos and music, blameless joys,
Innocent of questions
And beyond answers.
For I, Solitude, am thine own Self:
I, Nothingness, am thy All.
I, Silence, am thy Amen.

THOMAS MERTON

In dangers, in doubts, in difficulties, think of
Mary, call upon Mary. Let not her name depart
from your lips, never suffer it to leave your
heart. And that you may more surely obtain the
assistance of her prayer, neglect not to walk in
her footsteps. With her for guide, you shall never
go astray; while invoking her, you shall never
lose heart; so long as she is in your mind, you are
safe from deception; while she holds your hand,
you cannot fall; under her protection you have
nothing to fear; if she walks before you, you shall
not grow weary; if she shows you favor, you shall
reach the goal.

BERNARD OF CLAIRVAUX

Everything harmonizes with me, which is harmonious to you, O Universe. Nothing for me is too early nor too late, which is in due time for you. Everything is fruit to me which your seasons bring, O Nature: from you are all things, in you are all things, to you all things return.

MARCUS AURELIUS

The Prayer

Blessed be the year climbing its cliffs, the month
    crossing the fields
of hours and days, the bridges of minutes, the grass
    where we stood
that first moment, the festival music keeping our time,
    the hood
of the season's sky above us, the moment's fictive shield
against history, her tattered glance, her broken smile,
    everything real
or imagined, bless the rivers I invented to carry us, the
    woods
I planted as our own, bless even the sweet hurt, even the
    herd
of stars that trample my real heart which she has taught
    to heal.
Blessed be these trackless words running downstream
following the remote valleys she has cut through my life,
and blessed be the sounds they cannot make, but mean,
and blessed be all these pages watermarked with her name,
these thoughts that wander the unmapped roads of strife
and love, her blessed world whose dream is always a
    dream.

RICHARD JACKSON

Blessing at the Opening of a Business Meeting

Father in Heaven,
bless us as we gather today for this meeting.
Guide our minds and hearts
so that we will work for the good of our community,
and help all Your people.
teach us to be generous in our outlook,
courageous in face of difficulty,
and wise in our decisions.

Father,
we praise You,
for You are God for ever and ever.

Amen.

Prayer on the Six P.M. Subway

Unsteady my prayer mounts or falls why do
    I waste so want so O make room in the
    kingdom of light for lack lusters among the
    austere and severe for malfunction. only this to
    their crediters NO GREAT HARM DONE
    our passage writes MAYBE on water
nevertheless
might make it yet
who knows who knows
whether some hour
turns us on
unbelievable
as Christ's new somersaulting
start. his words his heart

    DANIEL BERRIGAN

The Prayer, Bless This Day

This day is full of beauty and adventure,
help me Lord to be fully alive to it all.
During this day, may I become a more thoughtful
    person,
a more prayerful person, a more generous and
    kindly person.
Help me not to be turned in on myself but
to be sensitive and helpful to others.
Let me do nothing today that will hurt anyone,
but let me help at least a little,
to make life more pleasant for those I meet.

When night comes, may I look back on this day
    without regrets;
and may nobody be unhappy because of anything
    I have said or done or failed to do.

Lord God, bless this day for me and all of us.
Make it a day in which we grow a little more like
    your Son,
and gentle as Mary His Mother.

Amen.

Collects: Contemporary, "Of a Saint"

Almighty God, you have surrounded us with
a great cloud of witnesses: Grant that we,
encouraged by their good example, may persevere
in running the race that is set before us, until at
last we may with them attain to your eternal joy;
through Jesus Christ, the pioneer and perfecter of
our faith, who lives and reigns with you and the
Holy Spirit, one God, for ever and ever.

Amen.

BOOK OF COMMON PRAYER

Living in Love

God of mercy, God of love,
it is sometimes difficult—
so painfully difficult—
to sustain a harmonious home life,
to maintain a marriage
based on
true friendship and love.
Let never a hint
of argument, frustration or suspicion
cloud our relationship.
We need
an extra measure of compassion
to understand
and to care for one another
with genuine sensitivity
and with open acceptance.
Let abundant peace fill our home.

REBBE NACHMAN OF BRESLOV

Blessing of a Household

May God, the Father of goodness,
who commanded us to help one another
as brothers and sisters,
bless this building with his presence
and look kindly on all who enter here.

Amen.

Blessing of a Vehicle (Or a Wagon)

Be gracious,
O Lord God,
to our prayers
and bless this vehicle with Thy right hand.
Send Thy holy angels to accompany it
that they may keep from all evils
those who ride in it;
and as once Thou didst grant faith and grace
through Thy deacon Philip
to the Ethiopian riding in his chariot
and reading the word of God,
so now show the way of salvation
to Thy servants that,
always given to good works,
they attain to everlasting joys
after the vicissitudes of the journey
and of this life.
Through Christ our Lord.

Amen.

Prayer for Our Daughters

May they never be lonely at parties
Or wait for mail from people they haven't written
Or still in middle age ask God for favors
Or forbid their children things they were never
    forbidden.

May hatred be like a habit they never developed
And can't see the point of, like gambling or heavy
    drinking.
If they forget themselves, may it be in music
Or the kind of prayer that makes a garden of
    thinking.

May they enter the coming century
Like swans under a bridge into enchantment
And take with them enough of this century
To assure their grandchildren it really happened.

May they find a place to love, without nostalgia
For some place else that they can never go back to.
And may they find themselves, as we have found
    them,
Complete at each stage of their lives, each part
    they add to.

May they be themselves, long after we've stopped
    watching.
May they return from every kind of suffering
(Except the last, which doesn't bear repeating)
And be themselves again, both blessed and
    blessing.

MARK JARMAN

Prayer for Men for Father's Day
A Twenty-First Century Liturgy Resource

O Lord Our Heavenly Father:
You, who adopt orphan children and care for the
  widows;
You stand at the door staring at the horizon,
desiring that your prodigal children come home.
Bless fathers and men everywhere this day
that the orphans may have role models,
that the widows may be provided what they need,
that the future men may see Christ reflected in
  the love
of piggy-back rides and hard-learned lessons
Through Christ and the Spirit to the Father.

Amen.

REV. NATHAN DECKER

Turning the Negative Tide

The news is such a downer!

Another bomb blast. More killed. The old hot spots are hot again.

Jesus blessed the peacemakers,

but we've still got a lot of work to do!

God, how I wish that happy endings came in life like we see them in movies! How I wish the good guys would win!

I admit that all this evil makes me mad. The violence makes me want to strike out, too. I admit it: I'm afraid. The other side is cheating and I'm tempted to cheat, too.

God, bless the peacemakers once again.

Remind us of your goodness.

Remind us of your sacrificial love.

Your way is faithful love, not breaking all the rules and lashing out.

Help me to find my own way back to faithful love.

Help what I say and do today turn the negative tide into a positive surprise.

Inspire me. Inspire all the peacemakers working around me—and bless those so far away that I only glimpse them responding, when that next headline breaks.

REV. DR. DANIEL BUTTRY

In Thanks

My God,
it has taken me time,
but I'm finally learning
to trust You.
When I called, You answered;
when I cried, You sent relief;
when I was in need,
You came through.
You are there for me
in every instance.
I need only
look, think, and understand,
and I can always find You;
there You are,
always ready to help.
Thank You, God,
for waiting for me.

REBBE NACHMAN OF BRESLOV

Prayer for a Marriage

When we are old one night and the moon
arcs over the house like an antique
China saucer and the teacup sun

follows somewhere far behind
I hope the stars deepen to a shine
so bright you could read by it

if you liked and the sadness
we will have known go away
for awhile—in this hour or two

before sleep—and that we kiss
standing in the kitchen not fighting
gravity so much as embodying

its sweet force, and I hope we kiss
like we do today knowing so much
good is said in this primitive tongue

from the wild first surprising ones
to the lower dizzy ten thousand
infinitely slower ones—and I hope

while we stand there in the kitchen
making tea and kissing, the whistle
of the teapot wakes the neighbors.

STEVE SCAFIDI

A Prayer for My Daughter

Once more the storm is howling, and half hid
Under this cradle-hood and coverlid
My child sleeps on. There is no obstacle
But Gregory's wood and one bare hill
Whereby the haystack- and roof-levelling wind,
Bred on the Atlantic, can be stayed;
And for an hour I have walked and prayed
Because of the great gloom that is in my mind.

I have walked and prayed for this young child an hour
And heard the sea-wind scream upon the tower,
And under the arches of the bridge, and scream
In the elms above the flooded stream;
Imagining in excited reverie
That the future years had come,
Dancing to a frenzied drum,
Out of the murderous innocence of the sea.

May she be granted beauty and yet not
Beauty to make a stranger's eye distraught,
Or hers before a looking-glass, for such,
Being made beautiful overmuch,
Consider beauty a sufficient end,
Lose natural kindness and maybe
The heart-revealing intimacy
That chooses right, and never find a friend.

Helen being chosen found life flat and dull
And later had much trouble from a fool,
While that great Queen, that rose out of the spray,
Being fatherless could have her way
Yet chose a bandy-leggd smith for man.
It's certain that fine women eat
A crazy salad with their meat
Whereby the Horn of Plenty is undone.

In courtesy I'd have her chiefly learned;
Hearts are not had as a gift but hearts are earned
By those that are not entirely beautiful;
Yet many, that have played the fool
For beauty's very self, has charm made wise,
And many a poor man that has roved,
Loved and thought himself beloved,
From a glad kindness cannot take his eyes.

May she become a flourishing hidden tree
That all her thoughts may like the linnet be,
And have no business but dispensing round
Their magnanimities of sound,
Nor but in merriment begin a chase,
Nor but in merriment a quarrel.
O may she live like some green laurel
Rooted in one dear perpetual place.

My mind, because the minds that I have loved,
The sort of beauty that I have approved,
Prosper but little, has dried up of late,
Yet knows that to be choked with hate
May well be of all evil chances chief.
If there's no hatred in a mind
Assault and battery of the wind
Can never tear the linnet from the leaf.

An intellectual hatred is the worst,
So let her think opinions are accursed.
Have I not seen the loveliest woman born
Out of the mouth of Plenty's horn,
Because of her opinionated mind
Barter that horn and every good
By quiet natures understood
For an old bellows full of angry wind?

Considering that, all hatred driven hence,
The soul recovers radical innocence
And learns at last that it is self-delighting,
Self-appeasing, self-affrighting,
And that its own sweet will is Heaven's will;
She can, though every face should scowl
And every windy quarter howl
Or every bellows burst, be happy still.

And may her bridegroom bring her to a house
Where all's accustomed, ceremonious;
For arrogance and hatred are the wares
Peddled in the thoroughfares.
How but in custom and in ceremony
Are innocence and beauty born?
Ceremony's a name for the rich horn,
And custom for the spreading laurel tree.

WILLIAM BUTLER YEATS

A Song of Creation

I Invocation

O all ye works of the Lord, bless ye the Lord;
praise him and magnify him for ever.
O ye angels of the Lord, bless ye the Lord;
praise him and magnify him for ever.

II The Cosmic Order

O ye heavens, bless ye the Lord;
O ye waters that be above the firmament, bless ye the Lord;
O all ye powers of the Lord, bless ye the Lord;
praise him and magnify him for ever.

O ye sun and moon, bless ye the Lord;
O ye stars of heaven, bless ye the Lord;
O ye showers and dew, bless ye the Lord;
praise him and magnify him for ever.

O ye winds of God, bless ye the Lord;
O ye fire and heat, bless ye the Lord;
O ye winter and summer, bless ye the Lord;
praise him and magnify him for ever.

O ye dews and frosts, bless ye the Lord;
O ye frost and cold, bless ye the Lord;
O ye ice and snow, bless ye the Lord;
praise him and magnify him for ever.

O ye nights and days, bless ye the Lord;
O ye light and darkness, bless ye the Lord;
O ye lightnings and clouds, bless ye the Lord;
praise him and magnify him for ever.

III The Earth and its Creatures
O let the earth bless the Lord;
O ye mountains and hills, bless ye the Lord;
O all ye green things upon the earth, bless ye the Lord;
praise him and magnify him for ever.

O all ye fowls of the air, bless ye the Lord;
O all ye beasts and cattle, bless ye the Lord;
O ye children of men, bless ye the Lord;
praise him and magnify him for ever.

IV The People of God
O ye people of God, bless ye the Lord;
O ye priests of the Lord, bless ye the Lord;
O ye servants of the Lord, bless ye the Lord;
praise him and magnify him for ever.

O ye spirits and souls of the righteous, bless ye the Lord;
O ye holy and humble men of heart, bless ye the Lord.
Let us bless the Father, the Son, and the Holy Spirit;
praise him and magnify him for ever.

BOOK OF COMMON PRAYER

When you are troubled about anything, you
have forgotten this, that all things happen
according to the universal nature; and forgotten
this, that a person's wrongful act is nothing to
you; and further you have forgotten this, that
everything which happens, always happened
so and will happen so, and now happens so
everywhere; forgotten this too, how close is the
kinship between a single soul and the whole
human race, for it is a community, not of a little
blood or seed, but of intelligence. And you have
forgotten this too, that everyone's intelligence is
a god, and is an efflux of nature; and forgotten
this, that nothing is owned by you, but that his
child and his body and his very soul came from
nature; forgotten this, that everything is opinion;
and lastly you have forgotten that every one of us
lives in the present time only, and loses only this.

MARCUS AURELIUS

A Prayer in Spring

Oh, give us pleasure in the flowers today;
And give us not to think so far away
As the uncertain harvest; keep us here
All simply in the springing of the year.

Oh, give us pleasure in the orchard white,
Like nothing else by day, like ghosts by night;
And make us happy in the happy bees,
The swarm dilating round the perfect trees.

And make us happy in the darting bird
That suddenly above the bees is heard,
The meteor that thrusts in with needle bill,
And off a blossom in mid air stands still.

For this is love and nothing else is love,
The which it is reserved for God above
To sanctify to what far ends He will,
But which it only needs that we fulfill.

ROBERT FROST

Prostration

Not every religious tradition has a formal prostration practice, but they all have a variation of it in bowing. Bowing is as close to a universal human religious practice as any practice can be. Traditional Jews, Christians, Muslims, Hindus, and Buddhists all engage in some form of bowing. In Islam, prostration, *sujud* in Arabic, is the central act of the five-times daily prayer (*salaat*), and proper prostration requires that your forehead, palms, knees, and the base of your toes all touch the prayer rug.

While Jews bow continually during prayer, they don't generally prostrate themselves. Yet the Bible tells us that biblical Jews often "fell on their face" when praying to God. Even today it is customary in more observant synagogues for the rabbi and cantor to prostrate themselves during the Yom Kippur *Amidah* prayer in a manner similar to Muslims. On a daily basis observant Jews recite the *Aleinu* prayer containing the line, "We bend our knees, prostrate, and acknowledge our thanks," and bow deeply when doing so.

Though Catholics and Protestants often kneel in prayer, prostration is more common to Eastern Orthodox forms of Christianity. Prostration goes further than that in Islam, with the person lying flat on the floor with her arms stretched out from her sides.

Buddhists bow three times before and after their formal chanting and meditation sessions. The first bow is to the Buddha, honoring one's intent to become a Buddha oneself. The second is dedicated to the *dharma*, the teachings of the Buddha, and the third is dedicated to the *sangha*, the community of Buddhist practitioners. Buddhists kneel, and then lower their foreheads to the floor, with their forearms and elbows on the floor. Their hands are placed palm up about four to six inches apart, and their head is placed between the palms. When the head touches the floor, the palms are raised.

The kind of bowing I practice, and the kind I am suggesting here, is full-body prostration adapted from Tibetan Buddhism:

1. Stand with your feet together, and bring your hands together with the base of the palms and the fingertips touching one another.

2. Place your hands on the crown of your head and give thanks for a pure body, then on your throat to remind yourself to purify your speech, then on your heart to remind yourself to let go of resentments.

3. Gently drop to your knees, and stretch out your entire body on the floor, extending your arms forward, your hands still touching in the sign of thanksgiving.

4. Then bring your hands to the top of your head to acknowledge that it is God, not the ego, that is the greater reality.

5. Remain prone. You may choose to focus on your breath, or offer a prayer of thanksgiving or supplication. I tend to simply rejoice in the feeling of surrender. I am completely vulnerable in this posture, completely at the mercy of whatever is happening. And yet through it all I sense God's support.

6. When you are ready, stretch your arms out in front and push yourself up to the kneeling and then standing posture. Return your hands to your head.

7. Repeat the process as often as you wish.

RAMI SHAPIRO

Acknowledgments

Grateful acknowledgment is given to those who contributed to this volume, even if the contribution took the form of an e-mail describing what prayer means to you or topics you felt we should have explored in this book.

They include: Dwight H. Judy for reviewing an early draft of the manuscript and providing insightful, constructive feedback; David Crumm, founding editor of ReadTheSpirit magazine and books (www.ReadTheSpirit.com); Brian McLaren; Fr. Thomas Ryan; Robert Grayson; Rabbi Simkha Y. Weintraub; Russell McNeil; Rabbi Dennis S. Ross; Chaim Kramer; Mary Earle and Margaret D. McGee, who both collected feedback and contributions from the men in their congregations; Dr. Ron Wolfson; Kent Ira Groff; Linda Douty; Rev. Canon C. K. Robertson; Nancy Copeland-Payton; Joseph Kelley; Rev. Kate Wilson; Pastor Don Mackenzie; Dr. Benjamin Pratt; Rev. Dr. Daniel Buttry; Joel Blunk; Jane Vennard; Todd Smiedendorf; and Kay Lindahl.

About the Contributors

Abba Agathon was the Coptic Pope of Alexandria and Patriarch of the See of St. Mark (661–677).

James Allen (1864–1912) was a British philosophical writer known for his inspirational books and poetry and as a pioneer of the self-help movement. His best known work, *As a Man Thinketh*, has been mass produced since its publication in 1903.

St. Augustine of Hippo (354–430), also known as St. Augustine, St. Austin, or St. Augoustinos, was bishop of Hippo Regius (present-day Annaba, Algeria). He was a Latin philosopher and theologian from the Africa Province of the Roman Empire and is generally considered one of the greatest Christian thinkers of all time.

Marcus Aurelius (121 CE–180 CE) was Roman Emperor from CE 161–180. He was the last of the "Five Good Emperors," and is also considered one of the most important Stoic philosophers.

Daniel Berrigan is an American Catholic priest, peace activist, and poet.

Wendell Berry is an American man of letters, academic, cultural, and economic critic, and farmer. He is a prolific author of novels, short stories, poems, and essays.

John Berryman (1914–1972) was an American poet and scholar. He was a major figure in American poetry in the second half of the twentieth century and was considered a key figure in the confessional school of poetry.

Rebbe Nachman of Breslov (1772–1810) was the founder of the Breslov Hasidic movement.

Walter Brueggemann is an American Protestant Old Testament scholar and theologian and an important figure in Progressive Christianity. Brueggemann is widely considered one of the most influential Old Testament scholars of the last several decades.

Rev. Dr. Daniel Buttry is a full-time peacemaker with International Ministries of the American Baptist Churches. He and his wife Sharon live in an urban neighborhood of Detroit. He is the author of *Blessed Are the Peacemakers*, profiles of eighty men and women who risked making peace in the face of global conflict. He writes regularly for www.ReadTheSpirit.com.

Bernard of Clairvaux (1090–1153) was a French abbot and the primary builder of the reforming Cistercian order.

St. John Cassian (c. 360–435), John the Ascetic, or John Cassian the Roman, was a Christian monk and theologian celebrated in both the Western and Eastern Churches for his mystical writings.

Paul Claudel (1868–1955) was a French poet, dramatist, and diplomat, and the younger brother of the sculptor Camille Claudel.

H. Kent Craig is a poet, author, artist, photographer, and musician with many works published and shown over the past decades, drawing from a strong confluence of deep eclectic inspirations. He lives in Oklahoma with his life partner, Renata, and their two dogs, Freckles and Boomer.

Lama Sūrya Dās, whom the Dalai Lama affectionately calls the American Lama, is an authorized lama in the Tibetan Buddhist order and founder of the Dzogchen Center. He is the author of the bestseller *Awakening the Buddha Within* and twelve other books, including his latest release, *Buddha Standard Time: Awakening to the Infinite Possibilities of Now*. For more information, visit www.surya.org or www.askthelama.com.

Rev. Nathan Decker is the pastor of the Cheriton Charge on the Eastern Shore District and a clergy member of the Virginia Annual Conference.

St. Francis of Assisi (1181–1226) was an Italian Catholic friar and preacher. He founded the men's Franciscan Order, the women's Order of St. Clare, and the lay Third Order of Saint Francis.

Robert Frost (1874–1963) was an American poet. He is highly regarded for his realistic depictions of rural life and his command of American colloquial speech.

Kent Ira Groff, founding mentor of Oasis Ministries in Pennsylvania, is a spiritual companion for journeyers and leaders, a retreat leader, and an inspiring writer-poet. He is author of *What Would I Believe If I Didn't Believe Anything?*; *Facing East, Praying West*; *Honest to God Prayer: Spirituality as Awareness, Empowerment, Relinquishment and Paradox* (SkyLight Paths); among other books.

George Herbert (1593–1633), was a Welsh-born English poet, orator, and Anglican priest.

Gerard Manley Hopkins (1844–1889) was an English poet, Roman Catholic convert, and Jesuit priest, whose posthumous fame established him among the leading Victorian poets.

St. Ignatius Loyola (1491–1556) was a Spanish knight from a Basque noble family, hermit, priest since 1537, and theologian, who founded the Society of Jesus and was its first Superior General.

Richard Jackson's collections of poetry include *Half Lives* published by Autumn House Press and *Heartwall* which won the 2000 Juniper Prize. A professor of English at the University of Tennessee at Chattanooga, he has won Guggenheim, Fulbright, NEA, Witter-Bynner, and NEH Fellowships, as well as the Slovene Order of Freedom Medal for his literary and humanitarian work in the Balkans.

Mark Jarman is an American poet and critic often identified with the New Narrative branch of the New Formalism; he was co-editor with Robert McDowell of *The Reaper* throughout the 1980s.

Fr. Thomas Keating, OCSO, is a Trappist monk and priest, known as one of the architects of the Centering Prayer—a contemporary method of contemplative prayer that emerged from St. Joseph's Abbey in Spencer, Massachusetts, in 1975.

John Keats (1795–1821) was an English Romantic poet. He was one of the main figures of the second generation of romantic poets along with Lord Byron and Percy Bysshe Shelley.

Thomas à Kempis, CRSA (c. 1380–1471), was a canon regular of the late medieval period and the probable author of *The Imitation of Christ*, which is one of the best known Christian books on devotion.

Larry Kibby is a Wiyot American Indian who currently resides in Elko, Nevada. He has been writing poetry since the early 1900's, most relating to the Indian World and other activity revolving around reservation and Indian community life, traditions, culture, and beliefs.

Chief Yellow Lark was a Lakota Chief in the late 19th century. He translated several Lakota (Sioux) prayers into English.

Brother Lawrence (c. 1614–1691) served as a lay brother in a Carmelite monastery in Paris. Christians commonly remember him for the intimacy he expressed concerning his relationship to God as recorded in a book compiled after his death, the classic Christian text, *The Practice of the Presence of God*.

C. S. Lewis (1898–1963) was a novelist, poet, academic, medievalist, literary critic, essayist, lay theologian, and Christian apologist from Belfast, Ireland. He is known for both his fictional work, especially *The Screwtape Letters*; *The Chronicles of Narnia*; and *The Space Trilogy*, and his non-fiction works, such as *Mere Christianity*; *Miracles*; and *The Problem of Pain*.

Ted Loder led the First United Methodist Church of Germantown from 1962 to 2000 in acts of social justice through a ministry that challenged the mainstream. Rev. Loder is retired, but remains a prolific author and poet.

Nelson Mandela is a South African politician who served as President of South Africa from 1994 to 1999, the first ever to be elected in a fully representative democratic election.

John Masefield, OM, (1878–1967) was an English poet and writer, and Poet Laureate of the United Kingdom from 1930 until his death in 1967.

General Douglas MacArthur (1880–1964) was an American general and field marshal of the Philippine Army who was Chief of Staff of the United States Army during the 1930s and played a prominent role in the Pacific theater during World War II.

Thomas Merton, OCSO (1915–1968), was an Anglo-American Catholic writer and mystic. A Trappist monk of the Abbey of Gethsemani, Kentucky, he was a poet, social activist, and student of comparative religion.

D. L. Moody (1837–1899) was an American evangelist and publisher who founded the Moody Church, Northfield School and Mount Hermon School in Massachusetts, the Moody Bible Institute, and Moody Publishers.

John Henry Newman, DD, CO (1801–1890), was an important figure in the religious history of England in the 19th century. Originally an evangelical Oxford academic and priest in the Church of England, Newman was a leader in the Oxford Movement.

John Philip Newell is a poet, author, and peacemaker. He is internationally acclaimed for his work in the field of Celtic spirituality, including his best known titles *Listening for the Heartbeat of God* and *Christ of the Celts*, as well as his poetic book of prayer *Sounds of the Eternal.*

John O'Donohue (1956–2008) was an Irish poet, author, priest, and Hegelian philosopher. He was a native Irish speaker, and as an author is best known for popularizing Celtic spirituality.

Gordon Peerman is an Episcopal priest and psychotherapist in private practice, and an adjunct faculty member at Vanderbilt Divinity School, where he teaches seminars in Buddhist-Christian Dialogue. He is author of *Blessed Relief: What Christians Can Learn from Buddhists about Suffering* (SkyLight Paths).

Dr. Benjamin Pratt is a pastoral counselor, literary scholar, and longtime caregiver himself. He is the author of *Guide for Caregivers: Keeping Your Spirit Healthy When Your Caregiver Duties and Responsibilities Are Dragging You Down*. He writes regularly for www.ReadTheSpirit.com.

Thomas Ryan, CSP, is a Catholic priest and member of the Paulist Fathers. The author of twelve books, his works include *The Sacred Art of Fasting: Preparing to Practice*; *Soul Fire: Accessing Your Creativity* (both SkyLight Paths); *Interreligious Prayer: A Christian Guide*; *Four Steps to Spiritual Freedom*; and the DVD, *Yoga Prayer*.

Rumi (1207–1273) was a 13th-century Persian Muslim poet, jurist, theologian, and Sufi mystic.

Steve Scafidi is a poet and the author of *Sparks from a Nine-Pound Hammer* and For *Love of Common Words*, both from Louisiana State University Press.

Rami Shapiro, a renowned teacher of spirituality across faith traditions, is an award-winning storyteller, poet, and essayist. He is author of several books including *The Sacred Art of Lovingkindness: Preparing to Practice* and *Recovery—The Sacred Art: The Twelve Steps as Spiritual Practice* (both SkyLight Paths).

Alden Solovy is a liturgist, poet, teacher, editor, and writing coach, as well as an award-winning essayist and journalist.

Rabbi Chaim Stern (1930–2001), US Reform rabbi and liturgist, is acknowledged as the foremost liturgist of Reform Judaism.

Rabindranath Tagore (1861–1941) was a Bengali polymath who reshaped his region's literature and music. Author of *Gitanjali* and its "profoundly sensitive, fresh and beautiful verse," he became the first non-European to win the Nobel Prize in Literature in 1913.

Voltaire (1694–1778), or François-Marie Arouet, was a French Enlightenment writer, historian, and philosopher famous for his wit and advocacy of civil liberties.

Rabbi Simkha Y. Weintraub, LCSW, serves as rabbinic director of the Jewish Board of Family and Children's Services in New York, centrally involved in its New York Jewish Healing Center and National Center for Jewish Healing programs. He also maintains a private practice in Couples and Family Therapy, helping people with parenting, marital relations, health-related issues, traumatic bereavement, and other difficult life challenges. He is editor of *Healing of Soul, Healing of Body: Spiritual Leaders Unfold the Strength and Solace in Psalms* (Jewish Lights).

Walt Whitman (1819–1892) was an American poet, essayist, and journalist. A humanist, he was a part of the transition between transcendentalism and realism, incorporating both views in his works.

Spiritwind Wood's heart, soul, and ancestry belong to the Cherokee. He lives life in a constant attempt to love and protect all that is sacred around us.

William Butler Yeats (1865–1939) was a twentieth century Irish poet and dramatist. In 1923, he was awarded the Nobel Prize for Literature and, as a celebrated figure, he was indisputably one of the most significant modern poets and confounded expectations by producing his greatest work between the ages of fifty and seventy-five.

Credits

SkyLight Paths is grateful to the following authors and publishers for permission to reproduce the material listed below. These pages constitute a continuation of the copyright page. Every effort has been made to trace and acknowledge copyright holders of all the material included in this anthology. The editors apologize for any errors or omissions that may remain and ask that any omissions be brought to their attention so that they may be corrected in future editions. Please send corrections to:

Editors at SkyLight Paths Publishing
c/o SkyLight Paths Publishing
Sunset Farm Offices
Route 4, P.O. Box 237
Woodstock, VT 05091

James Allen, "As a Man Thinketh," originally published in 1902; public domain.

Saint Augustine of Hippo, excerpt from *Saint Augustine of Hippo—Selections from Confessions and Other Essential Writings—Annotated & Explained* © 2010 by Joseph T. Kelley. Published by SkyLight Paths, P.O. Box

Index of First Lines

I. The Earth is our Mother; care for Her   29

I. Wherever you are, sit comfortably and close / your eyes   57

A fool is happy   71

A leaf that has served its function   68

A man only begins to be a man when he ceases / to whine and revile   51

A noble and God-like character is not a thing of / favor or chance   9

According to Thy will: That this day only / I may avoid the vile   48

Ah! from how great bitterness of soul have you often / delivered me   67

Ah, my dear angry Lord....   5

Almighty God, you have surrounded us with a great
    cloud of witnesses   131

As I walk the trail of life   91

As a man thinketh in his heart, so shall he be   99

As kingfishers catch fire, dragonflies draw flame   10

Be gracious, / O Lord God   134

Blessed be the year climbing its cliffs   127

Bring your body into an upright and dignified sitting position   114

Brother. / I am not your rival   52

Build me a son, O Lord   101

Day after day, O lord of my life, shall I stand before /
    thee face to face?   28

Deep peace of the running wave to you	86
Direct us, O Lord, in all our doings with your / most gracious favor	41
Do not dwell upon the sins and mistakes	120
Even here though I myself am pursuing the same instinctive courses ...	92
Everything harmonizes with me	126
Expand my heart, Jesus	63
Father in Heaven, / bless us as we gather today for this meeting	128
First, "I will deliver."	108
Follow my ways and I will lead you	124
For since the beginning of the world	78
Forget your life. Say God is Great. Get up	20
Generosity cultivates life, strength, beauty, wit / and ease	112
Give me all of you!!! I don't want so much of / your time, so much of your talents and money	4
God, grant me the serenity to accept the things I / cannot change	81
God has created me to do Him some definite / service	15
God, I'm frustrated	21
God of mercy, God of love	132
Great Spirit	82
Great Spirit hear my call	39
Hashem: / Grant me the ability to be alone!	49
He who finds fault with others is himself in the / wrong	54
I bless the night that nourished my heart	55
I have never gone to sleep with a grievance / against anyone.	104
I need no assurances—I am a man who is preoccupied / of his own soul	44
I pray because I can't help myself.	30
I will be with him in trouble	107
I'm impatient, Lord	74
Imagine yourself as a living house	62

In dangers, in doubts, in difficulties, think of Mary   125

In one salutation to thee, my God, let all my senses /
    spread out and touch this world at thy feet   19

In the way of God thoughts count for little, love is / everything   119

It may be that when we no longer know what to do /
    we have come to our real work   37

It suffices me for attaining to all righteousness   96

It's not true that Your saints have won everything ...   6

Kind Father, I thank You for my home where / loved ones dwell   47

Lead, Kindly Light, amid the encircling gloom   94

Let us praise those fathers who by their own   97

Lord, I need you to be rougher with me   106

Lord Jesus, our brother   123

Lord, make me an instrument of your peace   18

May God, the Father of goodness   133

May He support us all the day long   121

May I be among those who are hard to provoke /
    and easy to appease   105

May it be Your will, Eternal One, our God and the /
    God of our ancestors   46

May they never be lonely at parties   135

My God, / it has taken me time,   139

My grandfather is the fire   22

My Lord God, I have no idea where I am / going   38

My Strength and my Song   103

Not every religious tradition has a formal prostration practice   149

O all ye works of the Lord, bless ye the Lord   145

O God of peace, who has taught us that in /
    returning and rest we shall be saved   95

O Holy One / I hear and say so many words   100

O little self, within whose smallness lies   72

O Lord Our Heavenly Father: / You, who adopt
  orphan children and care for the / widows   137

O! Thou God of all beings, of all worlds, and of / all times   69

Oh, give us pleasure in the flowers today   148

Oh Great Spirit / Of the Indian People / Hear my words   16

Oh, Great Spirit,/ whose voice I hear in the winds   110

Oh, Lord of the Dance   70

Once more the storm is howling   141

Out of the silence at the beginning of time /
  you spoke the Word of life   27

Parent of All: / You have blessed us with children   83

Prayer changes at every moment in proportion to   3

Soul of Christ, sanctify me   73

That night I addressed a meeting of African /
  township ministers in Cape Town   43

The following guidelines for practice come from Father /
  Thomas Keating   87

The news is such a downer!   138

The rain has held back for days and days   77

There were other joys to be found in their / company   26

This day is full of beauty and adventure   130

This is my prayer to thee, my lord—strike   113

Time is endless in thy hands, my lord   122

To God our Father   31

[To have Faith in Christ] means, of course, trying /
  to do all that He says   42

To her who gives and takes back all, to nature ...   111

Unsteady my prayer mounts or falls   129

We gladly confess: "The eyes of all look to you   12

We have come to heal wounds, to bind up the / brokenhearted   61

Were I God almighty, I would ordain, rain fall /
      lightly where old men trod   80

When psalms surprise me with their music   24

When the sunset of this miraculous life arrives   66

When we are old one night   140

When you are troubled about anything   147

While I do this grit / work   50

Who is the you I pray to?   13

What has anyone done to deserve your grace?   65

You are One split into many   11

Prayer / Meditation

Men Pray: Voices of Strength, Faith, Healing, Hope and Courage
Created by the Editors at SkyLight Paths
Celebrates the rich variety of ways men around the world have called out to the Divine—with words of joy, praise, gratitude, wonder, petition and even anger—from the ancient world up to our own day.
5 x 7¼, 192 pp, HC, 978-1-59473-395-6 **$16.99**

Sacred Attention: A Spiritual Practice for Finding God in the Moment
by Margaret D. McGee
Framed on the Christian liturgical year, this inspiring guide explores ways to develop a practice of attention as a means of talking—and listening—to God.
6 x 9, 144 pp, Quality PB, 978-1-59473-291-1 **$16.99**

Women of Color Pray: Voices of Strength, Faith, Healing, Hope and Courage
Edited and with Introductions by Christal M. Jackson
Through these prayers, poetry, lyrics, meditations and affirmations, you will share in the strong and undeniable connection women of color share with God.
5 x 7¼, 208 pp, Quality PB, 978-1-59473-077-1 **$15.99**

The Art of Public Prayer, 2nd Edition: Not for Clergy Only
by Lawrence A. Hoffman, PhD 6 x 9, 288 pp, Quality PB, 978-1-893361-06-5 **$19.99**

A Heart of Stillness: A Complete Guide to Learning the Art of Meditation
by David A. Cooper 5½ x 8½, 272 pp, Quality PB, 978-1-893361-03-4 **$18.99**

Living into Hope: A Call to Spiritual Action for Such a Time as This
by Rev. Dr. Joan Brown Campbell; Foreword by Karen Armstrong
6 x 9, 208 pp, HC, 978-1-59473-283-6 **$21.99**

Meditation without Gurus: A Guide to the Heart of Practice
by Clark Strand 5½ x 8½, 192 pp, Quality PB, 978-1-893361-93-5 **$16.95**

Prayers to an Evolutionary God
by William Cleary; Afterword by Diarmuid O'Murchu
6 x 9, 208 pp, HC, 978-1-59473-006-1 **$21.99**

Praying with Our Hands: 21 Practices of Embodied Prayer from the World's Spiritual Traditions *by Jon M. Sweeney; Photos by Jennifer J. Wilson; Foreword by Mother Tessa Bielecki; Afterword by Taitetsu Unno, PhD*
8 x 8, 96 pp, 22 duotone photos, Quality PB, 978-1-893361-16-4 **$16.95**

Secrets of Prayer: A Multifaith Guide to Creating Personal Prayer in Your Life
by Nancy Corcoran, CSJ
6 x 9, 160 pp, Quality PB, 978-1-59473-215-7 **$16.99**

Three Gates to Meditation Practice: A Personal Journey into Sufism, Buddhism, and Judaism *by David A. Cooper* 5½ x 8½, 240 pp, Quality PB, 978-1-893361-22-5 **$16.95**

Prayer / M. Basil Pennington, OCSO

Finding Grace at the Center, 3rd Edition: The Beginning of Centering Prayer *with Thomas Keating, OCSO, and Thomas E. Clarke, SJ; Foreword by Rev. Cynthia Bourgeault, PhD* A practical guide to a simple and beautiful form of meditative prayer. 5 x 7¼,128 pp, Quality PB, 978-1-59473-182-2 **$12.99**

The Monks of Mount Athos: A Western Monk's Extraordinary Spiritual Journey on Eastern Holy Ground *Foreword by Archimandrite Dionysios*
Explores the landscape, monastic communities and food of Athos.
6 x 9, 352 pp, Quality PB, 978-1-893361-78-2 **$18.95**

Psalms: A Spiritual Commentary *Illus. by Phillip Ratner*
Reflections on some of the most beloved passages from the Bible's most widely read book. 6 x 9, 176 pp, 24 full-page b/w illus., Quality PB, 978-1-59473-234-8 **$16.99**

The Song of Songs: A Spiritual Commentary *Illus. by Phillip Ratner*
Explore the Bible's most challenging mystical text.
6 x 9, 160 pp, 14 full-page b/w illus., Quality PB, 978-1-59473-235-5 **$16.99**
HC, 978-1-59473-004-7 **$19.99**

Sacred Texts—SkyLight Illuminations Series

Offers today's spiritual seeker an enjoyable entry into the great classic texts of the world's spiritual traditions. Each classic is presented in an accessible translation, with facing pages of guided commentary from experts, giving you the keys you need to understand the history, context and meaning of the text.

CHRISTIANITY

Celtic Christian Spirituality: Essential Writings—Annotated & Explained
Annotation by Mary C. Earle; Foreword by John Philip Newell
Explores how the writings of this lively tradition embody the gospel.
5½ x 8½, 176 pp, Quality PB, 978-1-59473-302-4 **$16.99**

Desert Fathers and Mothers: Early Christian Wisdom Sayings—
Annotated & Explained *Annotation by Christine Valters Paintner, PhD*
Opens up wisdom of the desert fathers and mothers for readers with no previous knowledge of Western monasticism and early Christianity.
5½ x 8½, 192 pp, Quality PB, 978-1-59473-373-4 **$16.99**

The End of Days: Essential Selections from Apocalyptic Texts—
Annotated & Explained *Annotation by Robert G. Clouse, PhD*
Helps you understand the complex Christian visions of the end of the world.
5½ x 8½, 224 pp, Quality PB, 978-1-59473-170-9 **$16.99**

The Hidden Gospel of Matthew: Annotated & Explained
Translation & Annotation by Ron Miller
Discover the words and events that have the strongest connection to the historical Jesus.
5½ x 8½, 272 pp, Quality PB, 978-1-59473-038-2 **$16.99**

The Infancy Gospels of Jesus: Apocryphal Tales from the Childhoods of Mary and Jesus—Annotated & Explained
Translation & Annotation by Stevan Davies; Foreword by A. Edward Siecienski, PhD
A startling presentation of the early lives of Mary, Jesus and other biblical figures that will amuse and surprise you. 5½ x 8½, 176 pp, Quality PB, 978-1-59473-258-4 **$16.99**

John & Charles Wesley: Selections from Their Writings and Hymns—
Annotated & Explained *Annotation by Paul W. Chilcote, PhD*
A unique presentation of the writings of these two inspiring brothers brings together some of the most essential material from their large corpus of work.
5½ x 8½, 288 pp, Quality PB, 978-1-59473-309-3 **$16.99**

The Lost Sayings of Jesus: Teachings from Ancient Christian, Jewish, Gnostic and Islamic Sources—Annotated & Explained
Translation & Annotation by Andrew Phillip Smith; Foreword by Stephan A. Hoeller
This collection of more than three hundred sayings depicts Jesus as a Wisdom teacher who speaks to people of all faiths as a mystic and spiritual master.
5½ x 8½, 240 pp, Quality PB, 978-1-59473-172-3 **$16.99**

Philokalia: The Eastern Christian Spiritual Texts—Selections
Annotated & Explained *Annotation by Allyne Smith; Translation by G. E. H. Palmer, Phillip Sherrard and Bishop Kallistos Ware*
The first approachable introduction to the wisdom of the Philokalia, the classic text of Eastern Christian spirituality.
5½ x 8½, 240 pp, Quality PB, 978-1-59473-103-7 **$16.99**

The Sacred Writings of Paul: Selections Annotated & Explained
Translation & Annotation by Ron Miller
Leads you into the exciting immediacy of Paul's teachings.
5½ x 8½, 224 pp, Quality PB, 978-1-59473-213-3 **$16.99**

Spirituality

Gathering at God's Table: The Meaning of Mission in the Feast of Faith
By Katharine Jefferts Schori
A profound reminder of our role in the larger frame of God's dream for a restored and reconciled world. 6 x 9, 256 pp, HC, 978-1-59473-316-1 **$21.99**

The Heartbeat of God: Finding the Sacred in the Middle of Everything
by Katharine Jefferts Schori; Foreword by Joan Chittister, OSB
Explores our connections to other people, to other nations and with the environment through the lens of faith. 6 x 9, 240 pp, HC, 978-1-59473-292-8 **$21.99**

A Dangerous Dozen: Twelve Christians Who Threatened the Status Quo but Taught Us to Live Like Jesus
by the Rev. Canon C. K. Robertson, PhD; Foreword by Archbishop Desmond Tutu
Profiles twelve visionary men and women who challenged society and showed the world a different way of living. 6 x 9, 208 pp, Quality PB, 978-1-59473-298-0 **$16.99**

Decision Making & Spiritual Discernment: The Sacred Art of Finding Your Way *by Nancy L. Bieber*
Presents three essential aspects of Spirit-led decision making: willingness, attentiveness and responsiveness. 5½ x 8½, 208 pp, Quality PB, 978-1-59473-289-8 **$16.99**

Laugh Your Way to Grace: Reclaiming the Spiritual Power of Humor
by Rev. Susan Sparks A powerful, humorous case for laughter as a spiritual, healing path. 6 x 9, 176 pp, Quality PB, 978-1-59473-280-5 **$16.99**

Bread, Body, Spirit: Finding the Sacred in Food
Edited and with Introductions by Alice Peck 6 x 9, 224 pp, Quality PB, 978-1-59473-242-3 **$19.99**

Claiming Earth as Common Ground: The Ecological Crisis through the Lens of Faith
by Andrea Cohen-Kiener; Foreword by Rev. Sally Bingham
6 x 9, 192 pp, Quality PB, 978-1-59473-261-4 **$16.99**

Creating a Spiritual Retirement: A Guide to the Unseen Possibilities in Our Lives
by Molly Srode 6 x 9, 208 pp, b/w photos, Quality PB, 978-1-59473-050-4 **$14.99**

Creative Aging: Rethinking Retirement and Non-Retirement in a Changing World
by Marjory Zoet Bankson 6 x 9, 160 pp, Quality PB, 978-1-59473-281-2 **$16.99**

Keeping Spiritual Balance as We Grow Older: More than 65 Creative Ways to Use Purpose, Prayer, and the Power of Spirit to Build a Meaningful Retirement
by Molly and Bernie Srode 8 x 8, 224 pp, Quality PB, 978-1-59473-042-9 **$16.99**

Hearing the Call across Traditions: Readings on Faith and Service
Edited by Adam Davis; Foreword by Eboo Patel
6 x 9, 352 pp, Quality PB, 978-1-59473-303-1 **$18.99**; HC, 978-1-59473-264-5 **$29.99**

Honoring Motherhood: Prayers, Ceremonies & Blessings
Edited and with Introductions by Lynn L. Caruso
5 x 7¼, 272 pp, Quality PB, 978-1-58473-384-0 **$9.99**; HC, 978-1-59473-239-3 **$19.99**

The Losses of Our Lives: The Sacred Gifts of Renewal in Everyday Loss
by Dr. Nancy Copeland-Payton 6 x 9, 192 pp, HC, 978-1-59473-271-3 **$19.99**

Renewal in the Wilderness: A Spiritual Guide to Connecting with God in the Natural World *by John Lionberger*
6 x 9, 176 pp, b/w photos, Quality PB, 978-1-59473-219-5 **$16.99**

Soul Fire: Accessing Your Creativity
by Thomas Ryan, CSP 6 x 9, 160 pp, Quality PB, 978-1-59473-243-0 **$16.99**

A Spirituality for Brokenness: Discovering Your Deepest Self in Difficult Times
by Terry Taylor 6 x 9, 176 pp, Quality PB, 978-1-59473-229-4 **$16.99**

A Walk with Four Spiritual Guides: Krishna, Buddha, Jesus, and Ramakrishna
by Andrew Harvey 5½ x 8½, 192 pp, b/w photos & illus., Quality PB, 978-1-59473-138-9 **$15.99**

The Workplace and Spirituality: New Perspectives on Research and Practice
Edited by Dr. Joan Marques, Dr. Satinder Dhiman and Dr. Richard King
6 x 9, 256 pp, HC, 978-1-59473-260-7 **$29.99**

Spiritual Practice

Fly-Fishing—The Sacred Art: Casting a Fly as a Spiritual Practice
by Rabbi Eric Eisenkramer and Rev. Michael Attas, MD; Foreword by Chris Wood, CEO,
Trout Unlimited; Preface by Lori Simon, executive director, Casting for Recovery
Shares what fly-fishing can teach you about reflection, awe and wonder; the benefits of solitude; the blessing of community and the search for the Divine.
5½ x 8½, 160 pp, Quality PB, 978-1-59473-299-7 **$16.99**

Lectio Divina—The Sacred Art: Transforming Words & Images into
Heart-Centered Prayer *by Christine Valters Paintner, PhD*
Expands the practice of sacred reading beyond scriptural texts and makes it
accessible in contemporary life. 5½ x 8½, 240 pp, Quality PB, 978-1-59473-300-0 **$16.99**

Writing—The Sacred Art: Beyond the Page to Spiritual Practice
By Rami Shapiro and Aaron Shapiro
Push your writing through the trite and the boring to something fresh, something
transformative. Includes over fifty unique, practical exercises.
5½ x 8½, 192 pp, Quality PB, 978-1-59473-372-7 **$16.99**

Dance—The Sacred Art: The Joy of Movement as a Spiritual Practice
by Cynthia Winton-Henry 5½ x 8½, 224 pp, Quality PB, 978-1-59473-268-3 **$16.99**

Everyday Herbs in Spiritual Life: A Guide to Many Practices
by Michael J. Caduto; Foreword by Rosemary Gladstar
7 x 9, 208 pp, 20+ b/w illus., Quality PB, 978-1-59473-174-7 **$16.99**

Giving—The Sacred Art: Creating a Lifestyle of Generosity
by Lauren Tyler Wright 5½ x 8½, 208 pp, Quality PB, 978-1-59473-224-9 **$16.99**

Haiku—The Sacred Art: A Spiritual Practice in Three Lines
by Margaret D. McGee 5½ x 8½, 192 pp, Quality PB, 978-1-59473-269-0 **$16.99**

Hospitality—The Sacred Art: Discovering the Hidden Spiritual Power of
Invitation and Welcome *by Rev. Nanette Sawyer; Foreword by Rev. Dirk Ficca*
5½ x 8½, 208 pp, Quality PB, 978-1-59473-228-7 **$16.99**

Labyrinths from the Outside In: Walking to Spiritual Insight—A Beginner's Guide
by Donna Schaper and Carole Ann Camp
6 x 9, 208 pp, b/w illus. and photos, Quality PB, 978-1-893361-18-8 **$16.95**

Practicing the Sacred Art of Listening: A Guide to Enrich Your Relationships
and Kindle Your Spiritual Life *by Kay Lindahl* 8 x 8, 176 pp, Quality PB, 978-1-893361-85-0 **$16.95**

Recovery—The Sacred Art: The Twelve Steps as Spiritual Practice *by Rami Shapiro;*
Foreword by Joan Borysenko, PhD 5½ x 8½, 240 pp, Quality PB, 978-1-59473-259-1 **$16.99**

Running—The Sacred Art: Preparing to Practice *by Dr. Warren A. Kay; Foreword by*
Kristin Armstrong 5½ x 8½, 160 pp, Quality PB, 978-1-59473-227-0 **$16.99**

The Sacred Art of Chant: Preparing to Practice
by Ana Hernández 5½ x 8½, 192 pp, Quality PB, 978-1-59473-036-8 **$15.99**

The Sacred Art of Fasting: Preparing to Practice
by Thomas Ryan, CSP 5½ x 8½, 192 pp, Quality PB, 978-1-59473-078-8 **$15.99**

The Sacred Art of Forgiveness: Forgiving Ourselves and Others through God's
Grace *by Marcia Ford* 8 x 8, 176 pp, Quality PB, 978-1-59473-175-4 **$18.99**

The Sacred Art of Listening: Forty Reflections for Cultivating a Spiritual Practice
by Kay Lindahl; Illus. by Amy Schnapper 8 x 8, 160 pp, b/w illus., Quality PB, 978-1-893361-44-7 **$16.99**

The Sacred Art of Lovingkindness: Preparing to Practice
by Rabbi Rami Shapiro; Foreword by Marcia Ford 5½ x 8½, 176 pp, Quality PB, 978-1-59473-151-8 **$16.99**

Sacred Attention: A Spiritual Practice for Finding God in the Moment
by Margaret D. McGee 6 x 9, 144 pp, Quality PB, 978-1-59473-291-1 **$16.99**

Soul Fire: Accessing Your Creativity
by Thomas Ryan, CSP 6 x 9, 160 pp, Quality PB, 978-1-59473-243-0 **$16.99**

Spiritual Adventures in the Snow: Skiing & Snowboarding as Renewal for Your Soul
by Dr. Marcia McFee and Rev. Karen Foster; Foreword by Paul Arthur
5½ x 8½, 208 pp, Quality PB, 978-1-59473-270-6 **$16.99**

Thanking & Blessing—The Sacred Art: Spiritual Vitality through Gratefulness
by Jay Marshall, PhD; Foreword by Philip Gulley 5½ x 8½, 176 pp, Quality PB, 978-1-59473-231-7 **$16.99**

About SKYLIGHT PATHS Publishing

SkyLight Paths Publishing is creating a place where people of different spiritual traditions come together for challenge and inspiration, a place where we can help each other understand the mystery that lies at the heart of our existence.

Through spirituality, our religious beliefs are increasingly becoming a part of our lives—rather than *apart* from our lives. While many of us may be more interested than ever in spiritual growth, we may be less firmly planted in traditional religion. Yet, we do want to deepen our relationship to the sacred, to learn from our own as well as from other faith traditions, and to practice in new ways.

SkyLight Paths sees both believers and seekers as a community that increasingly transcends traditional boundaries of religion and denomination—people wanting to learn from each other, *walking together, finding the way.*

For your information and convenience, at the back of this book we have provided a list of other SkyLight Paths books you might find interesting and useful. They cover the following subjects:

Buddhism / Zen	Global Spiritual	Monasticism
Catholicism	Perspectives	Mysticism
Children's Books	Gnosticism	Poetry
Christianity	Hinduism /	Prayer
Comparative	Vedanta	Religious Etiquette
Religion	Inspiration	Retirement
Current Events	Islam / Sufism	Spiritual Biography
Earth-Based	Judaism	Spiritual Direction
Spirituality	Kabbalah	Spirituality
Enneagram	Meditation	Women's Interest
	Midrash Fiction	Worship

Or phone, fax, mail or e-mail to: SKYLIGHT PATHS Publishing
Sunset Farm Offices, Route 4 • P.O. Box 237 • Woodstock, Vermont 05091
Tel: (802) 457-4000 • Fax: (802) 457-4004 • www.skylightpaths.com
Credit card orders: (800) 962-4544 (8:30AM–5:30PM EST Monday–Friday)
Generous discounts on quantity orders. SATISFACTION GUARANTEED. Prices subject to change.